The Breakfast Book

The Breakfast Book

Diana Terry

with illustrations by Jean Saxby

MACDONALD & CO
London & Sydney

A MACDONALD BOOK

First published in Great Britain in 1984
by Macdonald & Co (Publishers) Ltd
London & Sydney

 A BPCC plc company

First published in 1983 by
Doubleday Australia Pty Limited
14 Mars Road, Lane Cove, NSW 2066

ISBN 0 356 10367 6

Macdonald & Co (Publishers) Ltd
Maxwell House
74 Worship Street
London EC2A 2En

ACKNOWLEDGEMENTS
Methuen Children's Books for permission
to reprint extracts from A. A. Milne's *Winnie The Pooh,
The House At Pooh Corner* and *When We Were Very Young*

Contents

Introduction

GONE are the days of Gargantuan breakfasts. Little more than a century ago, Charles Dickens wrote in *Dombey and Son* that one breakfaster 'not only arose next morning like a giant refreshed, but conducted himself, at breakfast, like a giant refreshing'. While the ingredients of breakfasts may have varied from country to country, the importance attributed to the meal itself did not change. Whether one was rich or poor, a hearty breakfast was consumed to fuel the body for the hard work or play in the day ahead.

Today our breakfast habits have changed. A hurried bowl of cereal or piece of toast, some fruit juice and a cup of coffee are standard morning fare. In these days of two wage earners, the cooked family breakfast of previous years is rare. And even rarer is the time to enjoy it.

After the rush and bustle of weekday mornings, who doesn't yearn for a chance to relax over a leisurely breakfast once in a while? It is for such people that this book is written. Whether you are planning a romantic breakfast for two, a casual gathering of friends, or even a more formal meal, you will find a complete menu just right for the occasion. You will also find that the menus, although impressive, are simple to reproduce and most of the preparation can be completed well ahead of time. With a minimum amount of last minute work required and a maximum amount of time to spend with your guests, you will have achieved one of the most important ingredients for successful entertaining: a relaxed host or hostess!

But, while this book is primarily designed to help you entertain friends over a relaxed, leisurely meal on special

occasions, don't neglect your daily breakfast. With a little thought and preparation you can fill your freezer with a variety of delicious foods: rolls, muffins, croissants or even quiches. Just a few minutes with the oven on while you're dressing for work and you have an instant and appetizing breakfast certain to dispel any morning blues.

To ensure a successful breakfast using the menus in this book, first choose your occasion, then gather around you some good friends. If you can't think of a special occasion, simply make one up! Begin mid to late morning, allowing yourself time for the final preparations and your guests time to arrive without an early morning rush. Then relax and let conversation flow while both you and your friends enjoy a tasty and wholesome meal in a convivial atmosphere.

1

Pancakes

PANCAKE making is thought to be one of the oldest forms of cooking. Traditionally eaten on Shrove, or Pancake, Tuesday and topped with sugar and lemon juice, pancakes are certainly not limited to this one day. Nearly every country has its own specialty, from the delicate French crêpes to the more substantial varieties of the British Isles and Scandinavia.

Topped or filled, sweet or savoury, they can be eaten as an entrée, main course or dessert — or as a substantial and wholesome breakfast. Serve them simply with fresh fruit, honey or syrup, or add some fried eggs, bacon and sausages. You can even combine both sweet and savoury in one serving, a style popular in Canada and the United States: maple syrup poured over the pancakes with a side serving of sausages or bacon provides an unusual and delightful treat.

Here are several pancake menus to try. Some are old, some are new; all are easy to prepare and with their accompaniments create a stunning effect. Most batters can be mixed long before your guests arrive. Accompaniments can often be made days ahead and set attractively on the table in advance. When guests arrive all that is required is to pour everyone a drink and let conversation flow while the final cooking is completed — a perfect recipe for relaxed and successful entertaining.

MENU FOR 4

Strawberry Whip

Avocado Pancakes
Grilled Bacon
Maple Syrup

Coffee
Cheese Platter
Fresh Fruits

THIS is an Australian version of the traditional American breakfast. Avocado pancakes are deliciously light with a slightly sweet and nutty flavour. Pour maple syrup generously over the top and accompany them with crisply cooked bacon. Begin with chilled strawberry whip and finish with a platter of cheese and fresh fruits for a colourful, tasty and healthy start to the day.

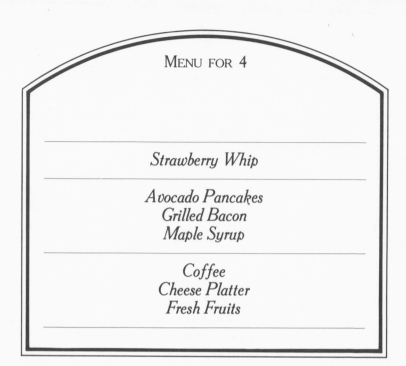

'But since he stood for England
And knew what England means,
Unless you give him bacon
You cannot give him beans.'
G. K. Chesterton, *The Englishman*

Strawberry Whip

1 punnet strawberries   *1 cup chilled evaporated milk*

1 Wash and hull the strawberries. Place in a blender or food processor
bowl and blend till almost smooth.
2 Add the very cold evaporated milk and blend for a few seconds. Pour
the frothy mixture into tall glasses and serve immediately. This drink is
quite thick: you may like to offer spoons to ensure that none is wasted.

Avocado Pancakes

1 small avocado (1/2 cup mashed)   *1 cup wholemeal flour*
2 eggs   *1/2 cup wheatgerm*
1 1/2 cups buttermilk or milk   *2 tsp baking powder*
* soured with 1 tbsp lemon juice*   *1/2 tsp salt*

1 Lightly mash the avocado. Beat in the eggs and half the buttermilk in
an electric mixer or by hand.
2 Combine the dry ingredients and beat into the avocado mixture with
the remaining buttermilk. Pour into a jug.
3 Heat a griddle or frying pan and grease lightly. Pour in about 1/3 cup
pancake batter and cook over a moderate heat until just beginning to set
around the edges and bubbles appear. Turn and cook 1 to 2 minutes on
the other side. Keep warm in a low oven till all the pancakes are cooked.
Makes about 12 pancakes.

Grilled Bacon
When the pancakes are almost ready, grill 8 rashers of bacon. Place on
a serving dish with the pancakes and take to the table.

Maple Syrup
Place a jug or two of maple syrup on the table and let guests help
themselves.

Orange Juice with a Difference

Cottage Cheese and Walnut Pancakes
Bacon Curls
Maple Syrup
Rum Butter
Apricot Honey

Coffee
Muscatels, Brie and Pumpernickel

HERE is another variation of that popular American breakfast. Pancakes are made with cottage cheese and wholemeal flour, and flavoured with cinnamon and crunchy chopped walnuts. Grilled bacon and slurps of maple syrup are a must. But try also generous dollops of rum butter and apricot honey. Both are easy to make and what you don't use today can be spread over croissants or toast to improve any breakfast. A dash of Grand Marnier added to your orange juice makes an excellent start to the day, while a creamy soft Brie on pumpernickel and some muscatels from your health food shop finish off the meal to perfection.

Orange Juice with a Difference

For each tall glass use:
2 to 3 ice cubes

1 tbsp Grand Marnier
orange juice

Place the ice in the glass. Pour over the Grand Marnier and top up with orange juice.

Cottage Cheese and Walnut Pancakes

1 tbsp butter
250g (8oz) creamed cottage
* cheese*
2 eggs
1 cup wholemeal flour

½ cup wheatgerm
1 tsp cinnamon
2 tsp baking powder
1½ cups milk soured with 1 tbsp
* lemon juice*
½ cup chopped walnuts

1 Blend the butter, cottage cheese and eggs for a few seconds in a food processor or beat well by hand until most of the lumps have disappeared.
2 Add the flour, wheatgerm, cinnamon, baking powder and 1 cup milk. Blend again till well mixed (you may need to scrape down the sides of the bowl). Add the remaining milk and blend for a couple of seconds.
3 Pour the batter into a jug and stir in the walnuts. Leave until ready to cook. (This may be prepared the night before.)
4 Lightly grease a griddle or frying pan. Pour in a well heaped table-spoonful of the pancake batter and cook over a moderate heat until bubbles start to appear and the pancake is beginning to set around the edges. Turn and brown the other side. Keep warm in a low oven while cooking the remaining pancakes.
Makes about 10 pancakes.

Bacon Curls
Just before the pancakes are ready grill strips of bacon, previously curled and secured with toothpicks. Scatter around the pancakes and take to the table. Serve onto warmed plates.

Maple Syrup
Place a jug or two of maple syrup on the table and let guests help themselves.

Rum Butter

125g (4oz) brown sugar
125g (4oz) unsalted butter
½ tsp cinnamon

1 tbsp fresh orange juice
4 tbsp rum

1 Cream the sugar and butter. Add the orange juice and continue creaming until very light and fluffy.
2 Add the rum 1 tablespoon at a time, beating well between each addition. Beat in the cinnamon. Chill. Rum butter keeps well in the refrigerator for several weeks. Bring to room temperature before serving.

> ' "It was the BEST butter," the March Hare meekly replied.'
> Lewis Carroll, *Alice in Wonderland*

Apricot Honey

250g (8oz) dried apricots
1 cup honey

2 tbsp brandy or apricot liqueur
(optional)

1 Cover the apricots with water and soak overnight. Drain.
2 Purée the drained apricots in a blender or food processor until almost smooth. Add the honey. Blend again until smooth and well mixed. Add the brandy or liqueur and blend for a few more seconds. Store in the refrigerator until ready to use. It will keep for months if given the chance!

> ' "No business before breakfast, Glum," says the King,
> "Breakfast first, business next." '
> William Makepeace Thackeray, *The Rose and the Ring*

Orange Juice

Blini
Ricotta Cheese
Yoghurt Cheese
Sour Cream
Caviar or Smoked Salmon
Spicy Sausage Platter
Brandy Cherries
Fresh Fruit Platter

Russian Caravan Tea

BLINI are traditional Russian pancakes usually served with sour cream and caviar or smoked salmon, or perhaps some sour cherries. Their delicious yeasty aroma, the unusual flavour of buckwheat, and a table laden with accompaniments provides a treat for all the senses. Place a colourful platter of seasonal fresh fruits in the centre of the table. Then add bowls of cheese and sour cream, plates of thinly sliced spiced sausage, and dishes of caviar or smoked salmon and brandy cherries. Your table will soon look as spectacular as your blini will taste.

Blini

1 sachet dry yeast (7g /¹/₄oz)	*2 cups buckwheat*
1 tsp sugar	*¹/₂ tsp salt*
3¹/₂ cups lukewarm milk	*3 eggs, separated*
2 cups wholemeal flour	*2 tbsp melted butter*

1 Mix the yeast and sugar with ¹/₂ cup of the milk. Stand for 10 to 15 minutes or until the yeast begins to froth.
2 Mix the flours and salt together. Beat in the remaining milk, the egg yolks and the melted butter. Then add the yeast mixture and beat well. (This step can be done by hand or in an electric mixer.)
3 Cover the mixture and leave until doubled in bulk. In Russia blini must rise for at least 6 hours, so prepare the batter the previous night and leave at room temperature until the morning.
4 Beat the egg whites till soft peaks form. Fold into the batter.
5 Preheat a griddle or heavy-based frying pan until a drop of water on it spits and sizzles. Pour on sufficient batter to make small pancakes 8–10cm (3–4ins) in diameter. Cook on both sides, smear with butter and stack on a serving plate in a low oven till all are cooked. Serve immediately.

'A good, honest, wholesome, hungry breakfast.'

Izaak Walton, *Compleat Angler*

Ricotta Cheese
Buy about 500g (1lb). This can be substituted for the yoghurt cheese but I prefer to use both, and so do my guests!

Yoghurt Cheese
Tip 1kg (2lb) good quality, chilled yoghurt into a piece of cheesecloth. Tie some string around the top and place in a strainer over a bowl for 8 hours to allow the liquid to drain off. Shape the cheese (now reduced to one quarter of its original size) into a ball, cover and refrigerate. The resulting soft, creamy cheese with a slight tang is well worth the very small effort required in making it. The quality of the final product depends on the quality of the yoghurt used.

Sour Cream
A 300ml (¹/₂pt) carton should be sufficient. Take to the table in an attractive serving bowl.

Caviar or Smoked Salmon

Pile the caviar into a bowl. If using thinly sliced smoked salmon, cut into strips and arrange on a plate with wedges of lemon.

Spicy Sausage Platter

Buy a variety of hot and spicy salami-type sausages. Thinly slice, arrange on a platter and decorate with spring onions.

Brandy Cherries

Use two tins of pitted cherries. Drain and cover with brandy. Leave overnight, then drain off the brandy and place the cherries in a serving bowl.

Fresh Fruit Platter

Buy fresh seasonal fruits, the more colourful the better. Leave whole or cut into large chunks and arrange on a glass platter.

To eat Blini

Spread some ricotta, yoghurt cheese or sour cream over a pancake. Top with any of the other accompaniments. Fresh fruit can be sliced onto a pancake or just eaten on its own while deciding what topping to try next. Be adventurous and experiment with different combinations of cheese, sour cream and other toppings. Share your discoveries!

This recipe will serve 10 to 12 hungry breakfasters. At a traditional pre-Lenten Russian feast, 15 delicate blini per person is a good number — fewer may be considered an insult to the cook! To serve larger numbers of guests, simply double the basic mixture. For large gatherings a blini meal makes a good buffet. Guests take a couple of small pancakes, a spoonful of cheeses and sour cream, and a selection of toppings. Then back for further experimentation.

Russian Caravan Tea

This tea can be bought from most delicatessens and some supermarkets. In Russia tea is made in a special samovar by the lady of the house. A small amount of very strong tea is poured into each cup and then diluted to taste with boiling water. It is usually served black, perhaps with a slice of lemon. If a sweetener is desired some sugar or a spoonful of sweet preserve is added to the cup.

Pawpaw and Coconut Milk Whip

Cornmeal Pancakes
Chilli Butter
Chicken Sausages
Bacon Bananas

Coffee
Fresh Fruit and Nuts

HERE'S a friendly, informal menu. Guests join you in the kitchen, sipping icy-cold pawpaw and coconut milk whip while you cook the pancakes, sausages and bananas. Or, better still, give everyone a job to do. Then pile everything onto a large platter, take it straight to the table and help yourselves. The slightly nutty taste of pancakes, spread with fiery hot chilli butter, teams well with the spicy sausages and the salty sweetness of the bacon bananas. Finish off with a colourful plate of chilled tropical fruits, a mixture of fresh nuts and piping hot coffee.

18

Pawpaw and Coconut Milk Whip

750g (1 lb 8oz) ripe pawpaw
(seeded and peeled)

1½ cups coconut milk
6 ice cubes

Purée the pawpaw in a blender or food processor. Add the coconut milk and ice cubes, and blend again till well mixed and the ice cubes are slightly crushed. Pour into tall glasses and drink through thick straws.

Cornmeal Pancakes

1 cup polenta (yellow cornmeal)
½ cup wholemeal flour
½ tsp salt
1 tsp cinnamon

2 tsp baking powder
2 tbsp vegetable oil
2 eggs, separated
1½ cups buttermilk

1 Combine the dry ingredients in a bowl.
2 Beat in the buttermilk, egg yolks and vegetable oil. Set aside. (This much may be done the night before.)
3 Just before cooking, beat the egg whites till frothy and fold into the pancake batter.
4 Cook 1 tablespoonful at a time on a lightly greased, moderately hot frying pan. As the pancakes are cooked place them on a large serving dish in a warm oven.

'Beloved, it is morn!
A redder berry on the thorn,
A deeper yellow on the corn,
For this good day new-born:
Pray, Sweet, for me
That I may be
Faithful to God and thee.'

Emily Henrietta Hickey, *Beloved, It Is Morn*

Chilli Butter

100g (3¹/₂oz) butter   *pinch curry powder*
pinch garlic powder   *¹/₂-1 tsp sambal oelek*

Mix all the ingredients together, adding the sambal oelek to suit your taste (it is very hot). Place on a butter dish and decorate with a sprig of parsley. If made the previous day, cover and refrigerate until half an hour before required. Sambal oelek is a chilli paste available in small jars from most delicatessens and supermarkets.

> 'The King asked
> The Queen, and
> The Queen asked
> The Dairymaid:
> "Could we have some butter for
> The Royal slice of bread?"'
>
> A. A. Milne, *When We Were Very Young*, 'The King's Breakfast'

Chicken Sausages

Prick well and grill or fry while the pancakes are cooking. Place on a serving platter with the pancakes and keep warm. Chicken sausages are available from chicken shops and many delicatessens and supermarkets.

Bacon Bananas

6 small, firm bananas   *6 rashers bacon*

Remove the rind from the bacon. Wrap around the peeled bananas and secure with a toothpick. Grill on both sides until the bacon is cooked. Arrange on the platter with the pancakes and sausages and take everything to the table.

Apricot Shake

Oatmeal Pancakes
Orange Butter
Rookwurst Sausage
Grapefruit Jam
Honey
Cheese Platter

Coffee

LIKE most pancake menus, this one requires a minimum of effort on the part of the cook. The pancake batter is quickly mixed first thing in the morning, or even the night before, then set aside until it is time to cook. In Wales oatmeal pancakes are served with bacon, honey, jam, marmalade and cheese. Try making this grapefruit jam. And, of course, the honey is indispensable. Provide also a selection of cheeses: a good blue cheese, some pepper cheese and one of the creamier varieties will make a good start. If you add some water biscuits and fresh or dried fruit the cheeses can be enjoyed with your coffee as well. But you will probably find your most popular accompaniments are the orange butter, spread generously over the pancakes and eaten with slices of smoked sausage.

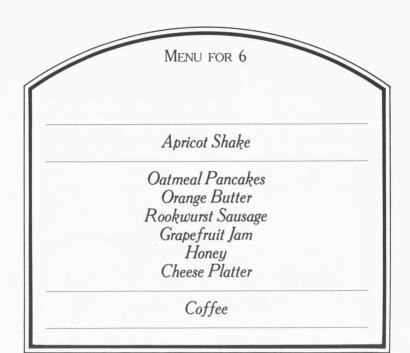

Apricot Shake

1 × 425g (14oz) tin apricots in nectar
1 ½ cups evaporated milk (very cold)   ½ tsp vanilla

1 Place the apricots and nectar in a blender or food processor bowl. Blend until smooth.
2 Add the evaporated milk and vanilla. Blend until very frothy. Pour into glasses and serve immediately.

'Drink, pretty creature, drink!'
William Wordsworth, *The Pet Lamb*

Oatmeal Pancakes   *very good*

1 ½ cups rolled oats   *1 cup wholemeal flour*
2 cups lukewarm milk   *½ tsp salt*
1 sachet dry yeast (7g/¼oz)   *2 + eggs, beat whites separately*
1 T ~~*1 tsp*~~ *sugar*   *1 tbsp vegetable oil*

1 Mix together the rolled oats and 1 ½ cups milk. Stir the yeast and sugar into the remaining ½ cup milk. Leave for 10 to 15 minutes until the yeast is frothy.
2 Combine the flour and salt and stir into the oatmeal mixture. Beat in the egg and vegetable oil. Add the yeast mixture and stir well.

'Isn't it funny
How a bear likes honey?
Buzz! Buzz! Buzz!
I wonder why he does!'
A. A. Milne, *Winnie The Pooh*

3 Cover the batter and allow to rise for at least 30 minutes or overnight.⟵
4 Drop tablespoonfuls of the batter onto a lightly greased, moderately hot griddle or frying pan and cook on both sides. Keep warm in a slow oven until all the pancakes are cooked. Makes 12 to 14 small pancakes — enough to serve, with the accompaniments, 6 very hungry people or 4 starving ones.

Orange Butter

125g (4oz) unsalted butter	*2 tsp finely grated orange rind*
2 tbsp brown sugar	*4 tbsp orange juice*

1 Cream the butter, sugar and orange rind.
2 Beat in the orange juice, 1 tablespoon at a time, until light and fluffy. Store in the refrigerator and bring to room temperature before serving.

Rookwurst Sausage

Follow the cooking instructions on the package. When the sausage is cooked, slice and pile into a heated bowl to serve. Rookwurst sausages are available at most delicatessens and supermarkets.

Grapefruit Jam

1 large grapefruit	*5 cups boiling water*	*1 kg (2lb) sugar*

1 Wash the grapefruit and slice thinly, removing the seeds. Place in a bowl, add the boiling water, cover and stand overnight.
2 Simmer the fruit and liquid in a large saucepan until the rind is tender, about 30 minutes.
3 Add the sugar and stir until it has dissolved. Bring to the boil and continue to boil, uncovered, until setting point is reached, about 45 minutes.
4 Cool for 10 minutes then place in warm, sterilized jars. Makes about 3 cups.

Based on Eggs

EGGS have long been a main-stay of breakfast in the English-speaking world. And why not? Packed into that small package is a wealth of goodness. One of nature's best sources of protein, the egg also provides a variety of vitamins and minerals essential for our health and well-being. Fortunately, eggs also supply flavour in abundance. Simply boiled or poached and accompanied by hot, buttered toast, they provide a repast few gourmets would reject. Or dress them up in any of a variety of ways — the possibilities are endless.

Whether you decide to serve your eggs plain or fancy, economical or with more extravagant embellishments, you will find them quick and easy to prepare. A few minutes in the kitchen will reward you with a tasty, nutritious and attractive meal.

In the following menus eggs form the basis of breakfasts designed to serve from as few as two to as many as twelve people. With an extra pair of hands to assist, the recipes can easily be adapted to cater for more should the occasion require it. Some of the menus are well suited to very casual entertaining, while others are ideal for those special occasions. All of them, however, are easy to prepare, allowing the cook to relax and enjoy the meal as much as the guests.

MENU FOR 6

Orange and Strawberry Juice

Prawn and Egg Ramekins
Wholemeal Avocado Muffins

Coffee
Fresh Fruit and Cream Cheese Platter

FRESH prawns and hard-boiled eggs are covered with a herby, mustard sauce and topped with melted cheese. The sauce should not be too thick, just sufficient to lightly coat each prawn and piece of egg. Any sauce left over can be scooped up with some wholemeal avocado muffin. Use a large platter of cream cheese and fresh fruits as a colourful and edible centre-piece for your table.

For more relaxed entertaining, the ramekins can be prepared ahead ready to pop into the oven with the muffins. Whip up the muffins when your guests arrive, or bake and freeze them a day or two before. Then merely thaw them in the morning and, while enjoying a leisurely glass of fresh strawberries puréed with orange juice, let them heat through in the oven along with the ramekins.

26
THE BREAKFAST BOOK

Orange and Strawberry Juice

1 ½ punnets strawberries | *3 cups orange juice*

1 Wash and hull the strawberries. Blend for a few seconds in your blender or food processor. Add the orange juice and blend again until fairly smooth. This will need to be done in 2 to 3 lots.

2 Prepare the juice before your guests arrive, pour it into a jug, refrigerate, then stir again before serving. If you really can't get hold of fresh strawberries, frozen ones will suffice.

Prawn and Egg Ramekins

6 hard-boiled eggs
200g (7oz) shelled, cooked
  prawns
2 tbsp butter
4 tbsp flour
2 cups milk

4 tsp grainy French mustard
4 tbsp finely chopped parsley
2 tbsp finely chopped chives
½ tsp salt
freshly ground black pepper
½ cup grated tasty cheese

1 Peel the eggs and cut into quarters lengthways. Divide the eggs and prawns evenly between the six ramekin dishes.

2 Melt the butter, add the flour and cook for 1 minute. Slowly add the milk, stirring continuously. Bring to the boil and cook until the sauce is slightly thickened. Remove from the heat.

3 Stir in the mustard, parsley, chives and salt. Check for seasonings and add the pepper as required. Pour the sauce over the prawns and eggs.

4 Sprinkle the cheese over the top and place under a preheated griller for a few seconds until the cheese just begins to melt. Do not let the cheese brown and toughen.

You may prepare the ramekins ahead of time then sprinkle with cheese and place on the bottom shelf of the oven to heat through while the muffins are cooking.

Wholemeal Avocado Muffins

1 egg	*1 cup wholemeal flour*
1 small avocado	*3 tsp baking powder*
2 tbsp castor sugar	*½ tsp salt*
1 cup wheatgerm	*1 cup milk*

1 Beat together the egg and avocado, which has been peeled, seeded and roughly chopped.
2 Mix the dry ingredients and fold into the avocado mixture with the milk until just combined.
3 Pour the batter into 12 greased muffin tins. Bake in a hot oven (200°C; 400°F) for 20 minutes. If you don't have muffin tins use 16 cup cake tins and bake for 15 minutes.

To reheat previously cooked muffins, place them in a slow oven (150°C; 300°F) for 15 minutes.

Fresh Fruit and Cream Cheese Platter

1 Cut a 250g (8oz) packet of cream cheese into cubes and pile into the centre of a glass platter.
2 Surround the cheese with bite-size pieces of fresh fruit, such as strawberries (the remaining half punnet from the juice), kiwi fruit, mandarin segments, slices of apple and pear (brushed with lemon juice to prevent browning), and rockmelon or pawpaw. In fact, use whatever fruits are in season at the time, being sure to include a good variety of colours.
3 Supply a number of toothpicks. Guests can skewer a piece of cheese with their selection of fruit.

'I'll fill up the chinks wi' cheese.'
R. S. Surters, *Handly Cross*

Fruit Juice

Individual Oven-baked Mushroom Omelettes
Cheese and Onion Muffins
Blue Vein and Tasty Cheddar Cheeses

Coffee
Dried Fruit and Nut Platter

HERE is another 'prepare-ahead' menu, quite different from the last-minute bustle usually associated with omelettes! Cook the almond and mushroom mixture and place it in the individual dishes well before your guests arrive. You can even lightly mix the eggs, milk and cream, then cover and set aside ready for a final stir before pouring over the mushrooms and baking. Mix the dry ingredients for the muffins, have the cheese, onions, milk and eggs all prepared. When your guests arrive hand them a drink, quickly and lightly combine the muffin ingredients and spoon into the prepared tins. Pour the omelette mixture over the mushrooms, put everything into the oven and sit back and relax for the next 20 minutes.

'I will make an end of my dinner; there's
pippins and cheese to come.'
William Shakespeare, *The Merry Wives of Windsor*

Individual Oven-baked Mushroom Omelettes

1 tbsp butter or margarine	*4 tbsp finely chopped parsley*
2 chopped rashers bacon	*½ tsp salt*
2 tbsp slivered almonds	*freshly ground black pepper*
400g (14oz) finely sliced	*6 eggs*
mushrooms	*¾ cup milk*
3 tsp fresh rosemary or 1 tsp dried	*¾ cup cream*

1 Melt the butter in a large frying pan. Add the bacon and almonds and sauté over a medium heat about 2 minutes.

2 Add the mushrooms and continue cooking, stirring frequently, until soft (about 5 minutes). Increase the heat and boil rapidly for a few seconds until all the liquid has evaporated.

3 Remove from heat and stir in the rosemary, parsley, salt and plenty of freshly ground black pepper. Divide the mixture evenly between 6 greased ramekin dishes.

4 Lightly beat together the eggs, milk and cream. Pour over the mushroom mixture. Cover and place on the lowest shelf in the oven. Bake in a hot oven (200°C; 400°F) for 20 minutes.

'The still hissing bacon and the egg
that looked like tufts of primroses.'
Benjamin Disraeli, *Coningsley*

Cheese and Onion Muffins

1 small onion	*½ tsp ground cumin*
1 cup wholemeal flour	*1 cup grated tasty cheese*
½ tsp salt	*2 eggs*
3 tsp baking powder	*1 cup milk*
1 cup wheatgerm	*¼ cup grated tasty cheese*
	poppy seeds

1 Chop the onion finely and sauté in a little butter until soft but not brown. Drain on absorbent paper.

2 Mix together the flour, salt, baking powder, wheatgerm and cumin. Stir in the grated cheese and sautéed onion.

3 Lightly beat the eggs with the milk. Fold into the cheese mixture until just combined.

4 Drop spoonfuls of the batter into well greased muffin tins. Sprinkle the tops with the extra cheese and some poppy seeds. Place in the oven above the omelettes and bake in a hot oven (200°C; 400°F) for 20 minutes.

'United Metropolitan Improved
Hot Muffin and Crumpet Baking
And Punctual Delivery Company.'

Charles Dickens, *Nicholas Nickleby*

Cheese

Provide a couple of cheeses as an extra accompaniment for the muffins. Stronger flavours such as those of Blue Vein and tasty Cheddar blend well with the already cheesy muffins.

Dried Fruit and Nut Platter

For a little bit of sweetness with your coffee offer a selection of dried fruits, such as dates, pears, apples and apricots or peaches. Some raw cashews and almonds, or any other nut you fancy, also make an excellent accompaniment.

MENU FOR 6
(or 2, or 4, or 8, or any number you like!)

Fruit Juice

Baked Egg and Onion Rolls

Coffee
Dried Fruit and Cheese Platter

TODAY ramekins usually refer to small ovenproof dishes used for baking eggs or other individual savoury meals. However, in previous centuries they described small pastry cases or hollowed out bread rolls baked with a cheese and egg filling. Hence, these Baked Egg and Onion Rolls are true ramekins in this earlier meaning of the word. Eggs are baked in the hollowed rolls over buttery, crunchy onion and topped with melted cheese. For maximum flavour, use wholemeal or mixed-grain rolls. It may take a little searching to find suitable ones but the final result will certainly be worth the effort.

Eat the hot, baked rolls with a knife and fork, accompanied by lightly sautéed mushrooms and tomatoes. Or, for more casual breakfasting, simply hand them around in large napkins. This way you can make the most of both the savoury filling and its edible baking dish, while enjoying a relaxed atmosphere and the knowledge of little washing up!

'Being kissed by a man who didn't wax his moustache
was like eating an egg without salt.'
Rudyard Kipling, *Soldiers Three (The Gadsbys)*

Baked Egg and Onion Rolls

6 round bread rolls
3 tbsp tomato paste
2 tbsp butter
3 finely sliced medium onions
1 tsp paprika

3 tsp carraway seeds (optional)
freshly ground black pepper
6 medium eggs
180g (6oz) grated tasty cheese

1 Cut a slice from the top of each bread roll and pull out most of the soft centre, leaving a shell 0.5–1cm (¼-½in) thick. Using the back of a teaspoon, spread some tomato paste around the inside of each roll.

2 Melt the butter in a frying pan, add the onions and cook until just beginning to soften (they must still retain some crispness). Divide the onions between the 6 rolls and sprinkle with the carraway seeds and a good grinding of black pepper.

3 Break an egg carefully into a cup and slide into a roll on top of the onions (using a cup ensures the yolk is not broken). Repeat with the remaining eggs and rolls. Top each egg with some grated cheese and a pinch of paprika.

4 Bake in a hot oven (200°C; 400°F) for about 12 minutes. The whites should be only just firm and the yolks still soft.

This recipe can be easily adapted to serve any number of people. For each 2 rolls, simply use 1 onion, 1 tablespoon tomato paste, 1 teaspoon carraway seeds, 2 eggs and 60g (2oz) cheese.

Dried Fruit and Cheese Platter

Place a selection of cheeses in the centre of a large serving platter. A soft, creamy Camembert, a nutty, sweet Swiss variety and a smoked cheese make a good starting point. Surround the cheeses with a variety of dried fruits and some pumpernickel rounds.

MENU FOR 4

Tomato Juice

Eggplant Ramekins
Olive Bread
Feta Cheese
Yoghurt Cheese

Turkish Coffee
Sherried Fruits

TRY this taste of the Mediterranean on a chilly morning. Layers of eggplant (aubergine), tomato, capsicum (peppers) and onion are cooked with a touch of oregano and olive oil, then topped with eggs and baked in the oven. Add a wholemeal soda bread with a handful of chopped olives folded through, some feta and a bowl of creamy yoghurt cheese. To finish, serve hot, sweet Turkish coffee and some dried fruits which have been marinated in sherry.

Tomato Juice

Pour straight from the can over some ice blocks. Add a couple of drops of tabasco to each glass, stir and serve.

Eggplant (Aubergine) Ramekins

500g (1 lb) sliced tomatoes	*1 sliced red capsicum (pepper)*
1 tsp salt	*1 sliced green capsicum (pepper)*
freshly ground black pepper	*250g (8oz) onions, peeled and*
1 tbsp finely chopped fresh	*sliced*
oregano or 1 tsp dried	*1 tsp paprika*
1 sliced medium eggplant	*⅓ cup olive oil*
(aubergine)	*4 eggs*

1 tbsp chopped parsley

1 Place the tomatoes in the bottom of a large saucepan. Season with some of the salt, a good grinding of pepper and one third of the oregano. Add the eggplants and season as for the tomatoes. Top with the capsicum, the onion and the remainder of the seasonings.

2 Pour over the olive oil, cover the saucepan and simmer for 40 minutes.

3 Remove the lid, stir and boil gently until nearly all the liquid has evaporated (40 to 45 minutes). Stir frequently to prevent burning.

4 Divide the boiling mixture between 4 ramekin dishes, make a slight hollow in the top of each and gently break an egg into each hollow. Sprinkle with paprika.

5 Cover and bake at 200°C (400°F) until the egg whites are barely set, about 8 minutes. Remove from the oven while the whites are still slightly runny: the very hot mixture will complete their cooking. Serve the ramekins immediately, sprinkled with parsley and accompanied by the hot olive bread, plenty of butter and the cheeses.

To save time in the morning, make the eggplant mixture the day before your breakfast. Then, simply reheat it in a saucepan before placing it in the ramekin dishes, adding the eggs and placing it straight in the oven as soon as the bread comes out.

Be sure to use olive oil: it just won't taste the same with a substitute. Remember to warn your guests that both the dishes and their contents are very hot.

You can also make this meal in a large casserole, making separate hollows for each egg. Serve from the casserole at the table.

Olive Bread

3½ cups wholemeal flour	1 tbsp butter
1 tsp bicarbonate of soda	2 cups buttermilk
1 tsp sugar	1 cup black olives, pitted and
½ tsp salt	chopped

1 Mix together the flour, soda, sugar and salt. Rub in the butter lightly. Stir in the buttermilk and olives until just combined.
2 With floured hands, quickly form the dough into a ball and place on a greased baking sheet, flattening slightly. Using a floured knife slash a cross on the top of the dough, cutting almost through to the bottom.
3 Bake in a hot oven (200°C; 400°F) for 30 to 35 minutes, or until the bread sounds hollow when tapped. Turn onto a wire rack while the eggs are cooking, then take to the table while still hot.

Feta Cheese
You can buy this from any supermarket or delicatessen. Serve it on a plate with some stuffed green olives.

Yoghurt Cheese
Follow the recipe given in Menu 3 of the Pancakes section (p. 16). Only half the quantity stated in that recipe will be needed.

> 'Werther had a love for Charlotte
> Such as words could never utter;
> Would you know how first he met her?
> She was cutting bread and butter.'

William Makepeace Thackeray, *Sorrows of Werther*

Turkish Coffee

Turkish coffee is traditionally made in a special long-handled copper or brass pot called an *ibrik*. However, a small saucepan will suffice. The coffee is served in very small cups and if second helpings are required a fresh pot is brewed. Each cup will contain a 'muddy' sediment which should not be drunk and is often used to 'read' the future. The strong, sweet liquid is topped with a creamy froth, equally distributed between the cups. A pinch of cardamom or cinnamon may be added with the ground coffee to give a subtle and delicious flavour.

4-6 tsp sugar	4 heaped tsp Turkish coffee
	4 demitasse cups water

1 Place the sugar and coffee in a Turkish coffee pot or small saucepan.
2 Add the water and bring slowly to the boil. As soon as the froth begins to rise, remove the pot from the heat and stir. Repeat twice.
3 Bring slowly to the boil again and remove from the heat without stirring. Pour the coffee into 4 small cups, a little at a time so that the coffee, 'muddy' sediment and froth are evenly distributed.

Sherried Fruits

200g (7oz) dried figs	200g (7oz) pitted dates
200g (7oz) dried apricots	medium dry sherry

Place the fruits in a jar, cover with the sherry and seal. Stand for at least one week before serving. When you have finished the fruit, don't throw away the liquid: pour it over another lot of fruit and start again.

'Why do they always put mud into coffee
on board steamers? Why does the tea
generally taste of boiled boots?'

William Makepeace Thackeray, *The Knickleburys on the Rhine*

Apple Juice

Poached Eggs in Mushrooms with Curried Crab Sauce

Wholemeal Popovers
Jam and Sour Cream or Yoghurt

Coffee

IGHTLY poached eggs nestle in large mushroom caps and are coated with sauce of curried crab in coconut milk. If suitable mushrooms are not available, don't worry: a bed of freshly cooked spinach is just as delicious. For a refreshing prelude, pour apple juice over crushed ice and float some mint leaves and a few sliced strawberries on top. Finish with crispy, golden popovers straight from the oven. Prepared earlier in the morning, they require only to be stirred, poured into tins and baked. Break open the hot popovers, without burning your fingers if you can, smother the steaming centres with jam and top with yoghurt or sour cream. A word of warning — large table napkins are essential to deal with these truly finger-licking treats.

'The rule is, jam tomorrow and jam
yesterday — but never jam today.'
Lewis Carroll, *Through the Looking Glass*

Poached Eggs in Mushrooms
with Curried Crab Sauce

6 large, firm mushrooms	½ tsp salt
2 tbsp butter	1 cup coconut milk
3 tsp curry powder	2 tbsp lemon juice
4 chopped shallots	1 × 200g (7oz) tin crab
1 tbsp flour	6 eggs
	½ cup grated tasty cheese

1 Wipe the mushrooms with a damp cloth. Brush the bottoms with oil, place in an ovenproof serving dish and bake in a hot oven (200°C; 400°F) while preparing the sauce and eggs.

2 Melt the butter in a saucepan and add the curry powder and shallots. Cook over a medium heat 1 minute. Add the flour and salt and cook 1 more minute. Remove from the heat and gradually stir in the coconut milk. Return to the heat and stir until boiling and slightly thickened. Stir in the lemon juice and crab, reheat gently, then cover and set aside whilst cooking the eggs.

3 Slide the eggs into a large frying pan of very gently simmering water. Cover and cook 2 to 3 minutes only. The whites should still be slightly runny: the hot sauce will complete their cooking.

4 Remove the mushrooms from the oven. Gently place a poached egg into each mushroom cap, cover with the sauce and top with the grated cheese. Place under a preheated griller for a few seconds to melt the cheese. Serve immediately at the table.

An alternative serving method is to assemble the mushrooms, eggs, sauce and cheese directly onto the plates. Pop each plate under the griller for a few seconds, then take to the table.

Wholemeal Popovers

1 cup wholemeal flour *2 large eggs*
pinch salt *1 cup milk*

1 Mix the flour and salt in a bowl. Beat in the eggs and milk to make a smooth, runny batter. Stand for at least 1 hour.

2 Pour the batter into 6 well greased brioche tins (for attractive, star-shaped popovers). Bake in a hot oven (200°C; 400°F) for 30 minutes, or until puffed and golden. Loosen the edges with a knife, turn out of the tins and serve immediately with jam and yoghurt or sour cream.

'Bread is the staff of life.'
Jonathon Swift, *Tale of a Tub*

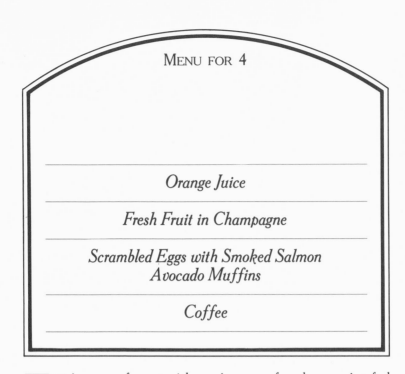

MENU FOR 4

Orange Juice

Fresh Fruit in Champagne

*Scrambled Eggs with Smoked Salmon
Avocado Muffins*

Coffee

T HIS is a menu for a special occasion — or for when you just feel like pampering yourself. Begin with a glass of freshly squeezed orange juice followed by fresh fruits in champagne. For extra panache serve the fruits in glass dishes or goblets then pour over the champagne at the table, allowing it to fizz and sparkle before your eyes. Continue in the same style with creamy scrambled eggs on a bed of smoked salmon, accompanied by delicate, light avocado muffins. Just halve the recipes given and you have the makings of a romantic champagne breakfast for two.

Fresh Fruits in Champagne

1 small rockmelon	*3 tbsp kirsch*
1 punnet strawberries	*½ bottle champagne*
2 kiwi fruit	*fresh mint leaves*

1 Cut the rockmelon in half and scoop out the seeds. Make as many balls as possible using a melon baller or cut the flesh into small cubes. Wash, hull and halve the strawberries. Peel the kiwi fruit, halve and slice thinly. Place all the fruit in a bowl, pour over the kirsch and refrigerate overnight.

2 To serve, arrange the fruit in small glass bowls or champagne goblets, spooning over any liquid. Decorate with a few mint leaves and take to the table.

3 At the table, pop the champagne and pour it over the fruit to fill the glasses.

Scrambled Eggs with Smoked Salmon

85g (3oz) packet sliced smoked	*2 tbsp butter*
salmon	*4 tbsp sour cream*
8 eggs	*cracked black pepper*
2 tbsp finely chopped chives	

1 While the muffins are cooking place the smoked salmon on heated plates. Keep warm.

2 Beat the eggs very gently. Melt the butter in a saucepan over a low heat. Add the eggs and stir with a wooden spoon until they are just beginning to set (3 to 4 minutes). Remove from the heat and stir in the sour cream.

3 Spoon the scrambled eggs over the smoked salmon. Sprinkle each serving with a pinch of cracked black pepper and some chives. Serve immediately.

Avocado Muffins

1 small avocado	1 cup milk
1 egg	2 cups plain white flour
2 tbsp castor sugar	½ tsp salt
	3 tsp baking powder

1 Mash the avocado with a fork, then beat in the egg and sugar. Stir in the milk.
2 Sift the flour, salt and baking powder. Stir into the avocado mixture until just combined.
3 Spoon the batter into 12 greased muffin tins. Bake in a hot oven (200°C; 400°F) for 20 minutes. These muffins can be served immediately or they can be frozen when cool and reheated on the day. To reheat, allow them to thaw, then warm through in a slow oven (150°C; 300°F) for 15 minutes.

'It's a very odd thing —
As odd as can be —
That whatever Miss T. eats
Turns into Miss T.
Porridge and apples,
Mince, muffins and mutton,
Jam, junket, jumbles —
Not a rap, not a button
It matters; the moment
They're out of her plate
Though shared by Miss Butcher
And sour Mr. Bate,
Tiny and cheerful,
As neat as can be,
Whatever Miss T. eats
Turns into Miss T.'

Walter de la Mare, *Miss T.*

Pineapple and Coconut Milk

Huevos y Chorizo (Scrambled Eggs with Chorizo)
Frijole Refritos (Refried Beans)
Avocado and Tomato Salad
Cornmeal Muffins

Spicy Hot Chocolate
Fresh Tropical Fruit

FOR a hearty breakfast try the hot, spicy flavours of Mexico. Eggs scrambled with chorizo are accompanied by those essentials of any Mexican meal: refried beans and avocado. Add a basket of golden cornmeal muffins and a jug of pineapple and coconut milk. Then, to finish in the style of a true Mexican feast, serve fragrant, foaming mugs of hot chocolate and chunks of chilled tropical fruit.

A major advantage of this feast, apart from its wonderful flavours, is the ease with which it can be prepared and served. Early in the week, make the hot, spicy chorizo sausage. Then, the day before your breakfast, cook the beans, mix the pineapple and coconut milk, and cut up the fruit. In the morning, combine the dry and liquid muffin ingredients in separate bowls, prepare the avocado and tomato salad, and relax until your guests arrive. All that is required then is to pour the drinks, mix the muffins, and pop them into the oven to bake while the eggs and sausage are scrambling and the beans reheating.

'Yet who can help loving the land that has taught us
Six hundred and eighty-five ways to dress eggs?'
Thomas Moore, *The Fudge Family in Paris*

Pineapple and Coconut Milk

1 × 420g (13oz) tin coconut milk
1 × 450g (15oz) tin crushed pineapple
1 × 250ml (8oz) tin unsweetened pineapple juice

Place the pineapple, pineapple juice and coconut milk in a blender or food processor. Blend until thick and smooth; you may need to do this in a couple of lots. Pour into a jug and chill overnight. To serve, pour into tall glasses over cubes of ice.

Huevos y Chorizo (Scrambled Eggs and Chorizo)

500g (1lb) chorizo sausage   *12 eggs*   *½ cup chopped shallots*

1 Place the chorizo in a large, cold fry pan. Turn the heat to medium and stir the sausage meat until cooked, about 10 minutes.
2 Lightly beat the eggs. Add to the cooked sausage meat with the shallots and scramble, stirring continuously, until the eggs are barely set. Transfer to a heated serving dish and take to the table.

> 'Give them great meals of beef and iron and steel,
> they will eat like wolves and fight like devils.'
> William Shakespeare, *Henry V*

Chorizo

Chorizo sausages can be bought at many continental delicatessens. Simply remove the skins before cooking. Better still, use the following recipe to make your own sausage mixture. It takes only a few seconds if you have a food processor and the taste is imcomparable.

250g (8oz) topside beef
250g (8oz) pork
1 small, roughly chopped onion
1 tsp salt
2 tbsp vinegar
½ tsp cinnamon

¼ tsp ground cloves
2 tsp chilli powder
1 tsp paprika
1 tsp cumin
1 tsp finely chopped fresh
  oregano or ½ tsp dried
2 peeled and crushed cloves garlic

1 Choose meat with some visible fat. Chop roughly and place with the onion in the food processor bowl. Process for a few seconds.

2 Add the remaining ingredients and process until a fine mince is obtained. Refrigerate until required (it will keep in the refrigerator for several weeks).

If you do not have a food processor, pass the meat, onion and seasonings through a mincer several times. Work in the vinegar with a wooden spoon.

'So munch on, crunch on, take your nuncheon,
Breakfast, supper, dinner, luncheon.'
Robert Browning, *The Pied Piper of Hamelin*

Frijole Refritos (Refried Beans)

2 cups dried red kidney beans
water
1 large, chopped onion
½ tsp cumin
2 peeled and crushed cloves garlic

1 tsp salt
2 bacon stock cubes
1 tsp chilli powder
4 tbsp fat (bacon fat if possible)
½ cup grated tasty cheese

1 Cover the beans with water and soak overnight.

2 Place the beans and water in a large saucepan, add the next 6 ingredients, cover and simmer until tender, about 2 hours. If necessary, remove the lid for the last half hour to allow some water to evaporate. When cooked, the beans should have a thick, soupy appearance.

3 Refrigerate the beans until ready to refry.

4 To refry the beans, melt the fat in a frying pan over a medium heat. Add the beans and mash slightly in the frying pan with a fork. Fry for a few minutes, stirring with the fork, until the beans form a thick, lumpy paste and are heated through. Turn into a heated serving dish, top with the cheese and take to the table.

Tinned beans may be used if desired. Simply fry the onions and seasonings for a few minutes before adding the undrained beans, then continue to fry as directed. However, by preparing the dried beans a day or two before your breakfast, no extra effort is required at the last minute and a better flavour is obtained.

Avocado and Tomato Salad

2 large avocados	3 tbsp lemon juice
2 large, firm tomatoes	3 tbsp oil
2 tbsp chopped fresh basil or 2	pinch salt
tsp dried	freshly ground black pepper

1 Halve the avocados, remove the seeds, peel and cut into small cubes. Chop the tomatoes roughly. Combine the avocado and tomato in a bowl and scatter the basil over the top.
2 Mix together the lemon juice, oil, salt and pepper. Pour over the salad and toss well. Leave at least 1 hour or prepare the previous day and chill overnight.

Cornmeal Muffins

1 1/2 cups polenta (yellow	1/2 tsp salt
cornmeal)	2 tbsp honey
1/2 cup wholemeal flour	2 tbsp melted butter
3 tsp baking powder	2 eggs
1 1/4 cup buttermilk	

1 Combine the polenta, flour, baking powder and salt in a large bowl.
2 Lightly beat together the honey, butter, eggs and buttermilk. Stir into the dry ingredients until just combined: the batter will still be a little lumpy.
3 Spoon the batter into 12 greased muffin tins and bake at 200°C (400°F) for 20 to 25 minutes. Place in a napkin-lined basket and take straight to the table. Provide plenty of butter.

Spicy Hot Chocolate

1 cup water
150g (5oz) roughly chopped
  cooking chocolate
5 cups milk

3 tbsp brown sugar
½ cup cream
½ tsp cinnamon
pinch nutmeg
8 cinnamon sticks

1 Heat the water. Add the chocolate and stir until dissolved.
2 Add the milk and bring slowly to the boil. Stir in the sugar.
3 Lightly whip the cream with the cinnamon and nutmeg. Pour the hot chocolate into 8 mugs and top with the cream. Hand around the mugs along with the cinnamon sticks to lightly stir in the cream.

'He hath eaten me out of house and home.'
William Shakespeare, *Henry IV*

Fruit Juice

Little Egg Pies
Ham and Basil Stuffed Tomatoes
Crabby Mushrooms

Coffee
Honey Rolls, Jam and Cheese

HERE'S an impressive buffet menu to serve 12 people. Eggs are baked over fresh herbs in little tart cases, tomatoes are stuffed with ham and basil, and the mushrooms have a golden, puffed filling of crab, cheese and pine nuts. Prepare both the tomatoes and the mushrooms the night before and refrigerate until ready to bake. The tiny tart cases can be made weeks before. Add a spoonful of herbs in the morning, then slide in the eggs and top with cheese just before cooking. Put everything in the oven at the same time, then take straight from the oven to the table.

Finish with the rolls, deliciously light with just a hint of honey. Made in the preceding days or weeks and then frozen, they require only reheating and some interesting accompaniments. Try a berry jam and some mild and sweet cheeses. Norwegian Ski Queen, Danish Grand Marnier and Peach Melba are hard to beat.

> ' "Oh, where are you going to, all you Big Steamers,
> With England's own coal, up and down the salt seas?"
> "We are going to fetch your bread and your butter,
> Your beef, pork, and mutton, eggs, apples, and cheese." '
> Rudyard Kipling, *Big Steamers*

Little Egg Pies
Almond Pastry

125g (4oz) butter	*pinch salt*
75g (2½oz) cream cheese	*½ cup ground almonds (use*
2 tbsp milk	*unblanched almonds, ground in*
1 cup wholemeal flour	*a blender or food processor)*

1 Have the butter and cheese at room temperature. Cream them well in the small bowl of an electric mixer. Beat in the milk.

2 Blend in the flour, salt and almonds on the lowest speed until just combined. Chill for 1 hour.

3 Divide the dough into 12 equal portions. Roll each portion into a thin circle, just large enough to line a lightly oiled muffin tin. Chill the lined tins for 1 hour.

4 Bake in a hot oven (200°C; 400°F) for 15 minutes, until lightly browned but still slightly undercooked. Leave in the tins for a few minutes to harden, then remove and cool on a wire rack. Store in an airtight container until ready to use; they will keep for several weeks.

You may substitute 60mm (2½in) vol-au-vent cases for the almond pastry. They lack that delicious nutty flavour but add a light, crisp texture.

12 tbsp finely chopped fresh herbs	12 small eggs
	½ cup grated tasty cheese

1 Place the tart cases on the serving dish with the Ham and Basil Stuffed Tomatoes and Crabby Mushrooms.

2 Place 1 tablespoonful of herbs in the bottom of each tart case. Press down slightly. Use a variety of herbs if possible, such as parsley, chives, tarragon, marjoram and rosemary.

3 Break an egg into each case over the herbs, being careful to keep the yolks whole. Top with some grated cheese, making sure the cheese covers the yolks.

4 Bake immediately in a hot oven (200°C; 400°F) for about 15 minutes, until the whites are just set and the yolks still soft. Take straight to the table.

Ham and Basil Stuffed Tomatoes

12 small, firm tomatoes	2 tbsp finely chopped fresh basil
2 tbsp butter	or 2 tsp dried
1 large, finely chopped onion	pinch salt
60g (2oz) finely chopped mushrooms	¼ tsp cayenne pepper
	pinch nutmeg
2 tbsp flour	1 egg yolk
¾ cup milk	6 tbsp fresh breadcrumbs
125g (4oz) finely chopped ham	2 tbsp butter
1 peeled and chopped clove garlic	

1 Prepare the tomatoes. Cut a thin slice from the stem end of each tomato. Scoop out the seeds and pulp with a teaspoon. Turn the tomatoes upside down on absorbent paper to drain.

2 Prepare the filling. Melt the butter in a saucepan. Add the onion and mushrooms (use the stems from the Crabby Mushrooms) and cook for 2 minutes. Add the flour and cook 1 minute. Remove from the heat and gradually stir in the milk. Return to the heat and bring to the boil, stirring until very thick. Remove from the heat again and stir in the ham, basil, salt, cayenne, nutmeg and egg yolk.

3 Fill the tomatoes with the ham and basil mixture. Top with the breadcrumbs which have been sautéed for a couple of minutes with the butter and garlic.

4 Place the stuffed tomatoes on a large, lightly greased ovenproof serving dish. Bake in a hot oven (200°C; 400°F) for 15 minutes.

Crabby Mushrooms

12 medium-size mushrooms   *1 egg*
200g (7oz) tin crab   *4 tbsp pine nuts*
½ cup grated tasty cheese   *few drops tabasco*
                pinch dried dill

1 Choose firm, white mushrooms with a good cup shape. Remove the stems and wipe the mushrooms with a damp cloth.
2 Mix together the remaining ingredients. Form the mixture into 12 small balls and place 1 ball in each mushroom cap.
3 Arrange the mushrooms on the serving dish with the tomatoes. If preparing the tomatoes and mushrooms the previous day, cover and refrigerate overnight.
4 Bake in a hot oven (200°C; 400°F) for 15 minutes: they will be puffed and golden when ready.

> 'The king was in the counting house
> Counting out his money;
> The queen was in the parlour
> Eating bread and honey . . .'
> *Tommy Thumb's Pretty Song Book*, 1744

Honey Rolls

1 tsp sugar
1 sachet dry yeast (7g / ¼oz)
½ cup warm water
1½ cups wholemeal flour
½ cup wheatgerm
2 tbsp powdered skim milk
1 tsp salt

1 egg
2 tbsp honey
¼ cup vegetable oil
½ cup water
¾ cup wholemeal flour
melted butter
cracked wheat

1 Stir the sugar and yeast into the warm water. Set aside for 10 to 15 minutes, until the yeast begins to froth.

2 Mix the first measure of flour, the wheatgerm, powdered milk and salt in the large bowl of an electric mixer. Add the egg, honey, oil and water, and blend together on the lowest speed.

3 Add the yeast mixture and beat at a medium speed for 10 minutes. Reduce power to the lowest speed and add the final ¾ cup flour.

4 When all the flour is incorporated remove the beaters and scrape down the dough from the sides of the bowl. Cover with plastic wrap and leave in a warm place until doubled in bulk, about 1 hour.

5 Stir down the dough and turn onto a floured board. Form into 20 small rolls and pack into a greased 27 × 17cm (11 × 17in) tin. Cover and allow to rise.

6 Brush the tops of the rolls with melted butter and sprinkle with cracked wheat. Bake in a hot oven (200°C; 400°F) for 20 minutes.

7 Serve immediately or cool on a wire rack and freeze. To reheat, place the thawed rolls in a slow oven (150°C; 300°F) for 10 minutes.

BASED ON EGGS

Ale
Tomato Juice or Grapefruit Juice

Kidneys in Marsala and Mushroom Sauce
Baked Eggs
Whole Baked Tomatoes
Bacon

English Breakfast Tea
Toast and Marmalade

HERE is a breakfast for those with a good appetite who like to begin their day in a hearty old English style. Juicy slices of kidney are served in a rich Marsala and mushroom sauce and accompanied by little circles of egg, whole tomatoes and rashers of crispy bacon, all baked in the oven. To maintain the true English tradition, begin your repast with foaming glasses of rich, dark ale. Or for the more faint-hearted, tomato and grapefruit juices can be offered. And to finish? Toast and marmalade, of course, followed by copious quantities of a strong, full-bodied tea. With such a breakfast under your belt, you will feel ready to face anything the day has to offer.

'Our breakfast consisted of what the squire
denominated true old English fare. He indulged
in some bitter lamentations over modern
breakfasts of tea-and-toast, which he censured
as among the causes of modern effeminacy and
weak nerves, and the decline of old English heartiness.'
Washington Irving, *Old Christmas*

Kidneys in Marsala and Mushroom Sauce

Kidneys make a perfect breakfast dish, requiring little preparation and a very short cooking time. To ensure a tender, juicy result, fry the whole kidneys in butter for just four minutes: they should still be pink inside. Then slice before adding to the sauce. Slicing before cooking can lead to the loss of those wonderful juices. And never, never let your kidneys boil: it makes them tough and stringy.

---

8 lamb kidneys
2 tbsp butter
4 chopped shallots
200g (7oz) finely sliced
mushrooms

2 tbsp Marsala
½ cup cream
pinch salt
freshly ground black pepper
chopped parsley

---

1 Prepare the kidneys. Cut out the small knob of fat and peel if necessary. Melt the butter in a frying pan. When it is nicely foaming add the kidneys and roll around in the hot butter for 4 minutes. Remove from the pan, cover and keep warm (they will cook a little further during this time).

2 Make the sauce. Add the shallots and mushrooms to the pan and cook over a moderate heat, stirring in the sediment from the kidneys, until the juices start to run (about 2 to 3 minutes). Add the Marsala and boil rapidly until only about 4 tablespoons of liquid remain. Stir in the cream, season with salt and pepper and boil gently for 2 to 3 minutes, until the sauce is slightly thickened and the flavours well blended.

3 Serve the kidneys. While the sauce is cooking cut the kidneys crossways into 0.5cm (¼in) slices. Remove the sauce from the heat, add the sliced kidneys and serve onto warmed plates. Sprinkle liberally with freshly chopped parsley.

BASED ON EGGS

While the kidneys are demanding your undivided attention the other dishes are taking care of themselves in the oven. The tomatoes can be entirely prepared the previous day, ready to put straight into the oven. Prepare the bacon first thing in the morning and place the eggs in their dishes, awaiting only the final touches before baking. As soon as the tomatoes, bacon and eggs go into the oven, begin preparing the kidneys and all will be ready to serve at the same time.

'Here is a devilled grill, a savoury pie, a dish of kidneys, and so forth. . . . Old Joe can give you nothing but camp fare, you see.'

Charles Dickens, *Dombey and Son*

Baked Eggs

6 large eggs	*extra butter*
2 tbsp butter	*cracked black peppercorns*

1 Use the first measure of butter to liberally grease 6 cocotte dishes. Break an egg into each dish. If preparing before your guests arrive, cover with a cloth and set aside until cooking time.
2 Just before cooking, sprinkle each egg with some cracked peppercorns and top with a small dot of extra butter.
3 Bake in a hot oven (200°C; 400°F) for 15 minutes: the whites should be barely set and the yolks still soft.
4 Remove the cocotte dishes from the oven, immediately run a knife around the edge of each dish and slide the eggs onto the warmed plates with the kidneys.

Whole Baked Tomatoes

6 small, firm tomatoes	*4 tbsp finely chopped chives*
½ cup mixed grain or wholemeal	*1½ tbsp butter*
* breadcrumbs*	*paprika*

1 Choose tomatoes which will stand without falling over. Cut a slice from the stem end of each tomato.
2 Sauté the breadcrumbs and chives in the butter for 1 minute. Press onto the cut surface of the tomatoes and sprinkle with a little paprika. Place on a lightly greased baking tray and set aside until ready to cook.

If tomatoes have been prepared the previous day, bring to room temperature before cooking.

3 Bake in a hot oven (200°C; 400°F) for 15 minutes. Place onto the warmed plates with the kidneys, eggs and bacon.

Bacon

Remove the rind from 12 rashers of bacon and snip the edges at intervals to prevent curling. Place the bacon on an ungreased tray and bake with the eggs and tomatoes.

Toast and Marmalade

Use a variety of breads for toasting: plain white, wholemeal and perhaps a mixed grain loaf. Toast after the main course has been eaten and bring to the table while still warm. Offer also a variety of marmalades. A good, dark tawny orange, a light, delicate lemon, and a mandarin or a three-fruit marmalade all demand some consideration.

'You may go to Carlisle's, and to Almack's too;
And I'll give you my head if you find such a host,
For coffee, tea, chocolate, butter and toast:
How he welcomes at once the world and his wife,
And how civil to folk he ne'er saw in his life.

Christopher Anstey, *The New Bath Guide (A Public Breakfast)*,
1766

Quiches and Soufflés

LIKE many of our favourite and best known dishes today, both quiches and soufflés had their origins in France. The quiche first made its appearance in the French province of Lorraine. There it consisted of a base of bread dough topped with any of a number of fillings, including the one we know so well as Quiche Lorraine. As time went on, the bread dough was replaced more frequently with a short-crust pastry. Today the variety of bases to choose from is almost as great as the variety of fillings.

Also offering any number of variations is the soufflé, based simply on a roux, fresh eggs and whatever flavouring you fancy. Although the original metal soufflé dish has now been replaced by china or earthenware, the characteristic shape, perfect for turning out light, airy soufflés, has been retained.

For breakfast, both soufflés and quiches are ideal — tasty, nutritious and easy to make. With most of the preparation being completed well in advance, they require no more than a last minute beat, stir or pour. You are then free to relax, sip and chat, while the oven does the cooking for you.

A further advantage of quiches and soufflés is the infinite variety of fillings, flavourings and accompaniments possible, allowing the imagination free rein. In the following menus, you will find both sweet and savoury offerings, some being perfect for casual entertaining while others are designed for those very special occasions.

Fresh Orange Juice

Plums in Port with Yoghurt and Cinnamon

Individual Crab and Smoked Salmon Quiches

Coffee
Fresh Fruit

A CRUNCHY, nutty pastry lined with smoked salmon, crab, chopped shallots and a scattering of flaked almonds makes these delicious little quiches. Begin with a glass of freshly squeezed orange juice. Then, while the quiches are cooking, serve a compote of plums marinated in port and topped with a dollop of yoghurt and a sprinkling of cinnamon. Hot, freshly brewed coffee and a bowl of fruit complete this very special breakfast.

Plums in Port with Yoghurt and Cinnamon

2 × 825g (1lb 10oz) tins dark   *12 tbsp port*
* plums*   *2 × 200ml (7oz) tubs yoghurt*
                          cinnamon

1 Drain the plums, cut in half very carefully and remove the stones. Divide between 6 small glass dishes. Pour 2 tablespoons port over each serving of plums. Cover and chill overnight.
2 Just before serving, top the plums with a dollop of your favourite creamy yoghurt and spinkle with a good pinch of cinnamon.

Individual Crab and Smoked Salmon Quiches

Almond Pastry

125g (4oz) butter   *pinch salt*
75g (2½oz) cream cheese   *½ cup ground almonds (grind*
2 tbsp milk   * unblanched almonds in your*
1 cup wholemeal flour   * blender or food processor)*

1 Have the butter and cheese at room temperature. Cream them well in the small bowl of an electric mixer. Beat in the milk.
2 Blend in the flour, salt and almonds on the lowest speed until just combined. Chill for 1 hour.
3 Divide the dough into 3 portions, then 2 of the portions into 3 equal pieces. Roll each of these 6 smaller pieces of dough into a thin circle just large enough to line a lightly oiled individual quiche tin. Place the lined tins on a baking tray in the refrigerator for at least 1 hour (or overnight). The remaining pastry can be used to line 4 muffin tins for the Little Egg Pies (see page 50).

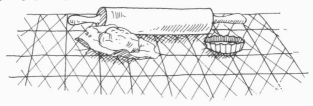

Crab and Smoked Salmon Filling

4 small eggs
¾ cup cream
2 tbsp mayonnaise
pinch salt
pinch mustard

freshly ground black pepper
85g (3oz) packet sliced smoked
  salmon
1 × 170g (6oz) tin crab
6 chopped shallots
½ cup flaked almonds

1 Prepare the custard. In a small bowl break up the eggs with a wire whisk — do not beat them. Stir in the cream, mayonnaise, salt, mustard and a good grinding of pepper. Pour into a jug.

2 Assemble the quiches. Place slices of smoked salmon in the chilled pastry cases. Sprinkle over the drained crab meat, then the chopped shallots. Carefully pour over the custard mixture and scatter the tops with the flaked almonds.

3 Bake in a hot oven (200°C; 400°F) for 10 minutes then reduce heat to 180°C (350°F) for a further 15 to 20 minutes. Remove from the oven and leave the quiches in the tins for a couple of minutes to set before serving.

The pastry for these quiches can be made as far ahead as you like and the lined tins frozen until the morning of your breakfast. Or prepare the pastry the day before and chill overnight. Prepare the custard before your guests arrive and have all the ingredients ready for the last-minute assembling and baking.

'There were three ravens sat on a tree,
They were as black as they might be.
Then one of them said to his mate,
"Where shall we our breakfast take?" '

The Three Ravens, *The Oxford Book of Ballads*

Orange Juice

Individual Prawn and Avocado Soufflés
Rapid Rye Rolls
Walnut Layer and Carraway Cheese

Coffee
Fresh Fruits with Almond Cream

L IGHT, fluffy avocado soufflés are cooked over a layer of prawns and served with rye-flavoured rolls, hot from the oven and smothered in butter. These rolls are very quick and easy to make; the electric mixer does all the kneading for you. Start them first thing in the morning and bake with the soufflés. Or cook and freeze them previously, ready to thaw and reheat. Add a walnut or carraway cheese to accompany those rolls remaining after the soufflés have been eaten. Then finish with coffee and chunks of fresh fruit dipped into almond-flavoured whipped cream.

Individual Prawn and Avocado Soufflés

butter
extra grated Parmesan cheese
150g (5oz) peeled prawns
1 large or 2 small avocados
¼ cup lemon juice

½ tsp salt
freshly ground black pepper
3 eggs, separated
2 tbsp chopped chives
1 tbsp grated Parmesan cheese

1 Grease 4 individual soufflé dishes with butter and sprinkle the sides with the extra Parmesan cheese. Divide the prawns between the 4 dishes.
2 Mash the avocado roughly with a fork and stir in the lemon juice. Then add the salt, plenty of pepper, the egg yolks, chives and the 1 tablespoon Parmesan cheese. Beat lightly with the fork: don't worry if some small lumps of avocado remain.
3 Beat the egg whites until firm but not dry. Fold 1 tablespoonful into the avocado mixture to lighten it, then quickly but gently fold in the remaining whites. Spoon the mixture into the soufflé dishes over the prawns, put straight into a hot oven (200°C; 400°F) for 12 to 15 minutes. Serve immediately.

These soufflés won't fail if you follow 3 simple 'don'ts'.
1 Don't overbeat the egg whites.
2 Don't overmix the whites and avocado mixture: some lumps of egg white won't mar the finished soufflé.
3 Don't overcook. In fact, the flavour is much better if slightly undercooked.

'O flesh, flesh, how thou are fishified!'
William Shakespeare, *Romeo and Juliet*

Rapid Rye Rolls

1 sachet dry yeast (7g/¼oz)
1 tbsp brown sugar
1 cup warm water
1 egg
1 cup rye flour

1 tsp salt
2 tbsp softened butter
1 cup wholemeal flour
¼ cup gluten flour
1 tsp carraway seeds (optional)
melted butter for glazing

1 Combine the yeast, sugar and water in the large bowl of an electric mixer. Leave for 10 to 15 minutes, until the yeast begins to froth.

2 Add the egg, rye flour, salt and butter and beat for 10 minutes at medium speed. Then add the remaining flours and the carraway seeds. Beat again until all the flour is incorporated.

3 Remove the beaters and scrape down the dough from the sides of the bowl. Push into a rough ball, cover with plastic food wrap and rest in a warm place until doubled in bulk (30 to 60 minutes).

4 Stir the dough down to its original size. Using 2 tablespoons divide it between 12 greased muffin tins. Press down well into the tins with the slightly damp back of a spoon.

5 Cover and leave to rise again until doubled in size, about 30 minutes. Brush with melted butter and bake in a hot oven (200°C; 400°F) for 15 minutes.

Gluten flour can be obtained readily from health food stores: it gives the rolls a good, light texture.

'Give me again my hollow tree
A crust of bread, and liberty.'

Alexander Pope, *Satire VI*

Fresh Fruits with Almond Cream

*125g (4oz) almond macaroons   300ml (½ pint) cream, whipped
large chunks of whatever colourful fresh fruits are in season*

Crumble the macaroons coarsely and fold into the cream. Pile into a glass bowl, place on a large glass platter and surround with the chilled fruit.

Almond Macaroons

*2 egg whites   1 cup ground almonds (use
pinch salt   unblanched almonds ground in a
½ cup castor sugar   food processor or blender)
                          1 tbsp cornflour*

1 Beat the egg whites and salt until frothy. Gradually add the sugar, beating until the mixture is very stiff and all the sugar is incorporated. Fold in the almonds and cornflour.

2 Drop small teaspoonfuls onto baking trays which have been greased and lightly dusted with cornflour. Dry out in a very slow oven (100°C; 200°F) for 1 hour. Leave on the trays for a few minutes, then cool on wire racks.

Almond macaroons can be bought at many delicatessens. However, the home-ground, unblanched almonds used in this recipe give a much nuttier flavour. Make the macaroons a few days, or weeks, beforehand; they keep well in an airtight container. This recipe makes about 36 small macaroons. Those not used in the Almond Cream can be served on another occasion with after-dinner coffee or to accompany home-made ice-cream.

Tomato and Grapefruit Juice
Chilled Fresh Fruit

Breakfast Chestnut Soufflé
Coconut-Corn Bread
Apricot and Almond Jam

Mocha Coffee

THIS soufflé, with its accompanying coconut-corn bread and apricot and almond jam, is not only both different and delicious — it can be completely prepared before your guests arrive. Make the chestnut and egg yolk mixture first thing in the morning or even the day before. Just refrigerate it overnight, then bring it to room temperature before proceeding. Add the beaten egg whites, pour the mixture into the prepared dish and cover with plastic wrap or a plate. The soufflé will remain light and airy for an hour or more. When your guests arrive you need only finish mixing the bread before putting both it and the soufflé into the oven. Then sit back and enjoy a refreshing glass of tomato and grapefruit juice, chilled pieces of fresh fruit and the conversation of your friends for the next 35 minutes.

'And they fell to breakfast with what appetite they might.'
Charles Dickens, *Dombey and Son*

Tomato and Grapefruit Juice

Combine equal quantities of tomato juice and grapefruit juice (freshly squeezed if possible). Chill well before serving.

'I am willing to taste any drink once.'

James Branch Cabell, *Jurgen*

Breakfast Chestnut Soufflé

3 tbsp butter	pinch nutmeg
3 tbsp flour	1 tbsp finely grated lemon rind
1 cup milk	½ tsp vanilla
½ x 440g (14oz) tin	6 eggs, separated
unsweetened chestnut purée	castor sugar
2 tbsp brown sugar	pinch salt
	flaked almonds

1 Melt the butter in a saucepan and add the flour. Cook for 1 minute. Remove from the heat and gradually add the milk. Return to the heat and stir until boiling and slightly thickened.

2 Cool a little. Stir in the chestnut purée, sugar, nutmeg, lemon rind and vanilla. Whisk in the egg yolks until smooth.

3 Grease a large soufflé dish (6 cup capacity) and sprinkle the base and sides with castor sugar.

4 Beat the egg whites with the pinch of salt until they are firm. Do not overbeat or they will be difficult to fold in. Gently stir a couple of tablespoonfuls of the beaten whites into the chestnut mixture, then lightly fold in the remaining whites. Spoon into the prepared soufflé dish. Scatter some flaked almonds over the top and bake in a moderately hot oven (190°C; 375°F) for 35 to 40 minutes. Place in the oven on a shelf below the coconut-corn bread.

'And he gave it for his opinion, that whoever could make 2 ears of corn or 2 blades of grass to grow upon a spot of ground where only 1 grew before, would deserve better of mankind and do more essential service to his country than the whole race of politicians put together.'

Jonathan Swift, *Gulliver's Travels*

Coconut-Corn Bread

1 cup wholemeal flour	*1 tsp cinnamon*
1 cup polenta	*2 tbsp sugar*
1 cup coconut	*2 eggs*
1 tbsp baking powder	*1¼ cups milk*
½ tsp salt	*2 tbsp melted butter*

1 Combine the dry ingredients in a bowl: this can be done well ahead of time.
2 Lightly beat together the eggs, milk and butter. Pour into the centre of the flour mixture and stir until just combined.
3 Pour the batter into a greased 20cm (8in) round cake tin and place in a moderately hot oven (190°C; 375°F) above the soufflé. Both the bread and the soufflé will be ready in 35 to 40 minutes.
4 Take the cooked bread to the table on a round board or cut into wedges and place in napkin-lined baskets. Provide plenty of butter to spread generously over the bread.

When the soufflé is finished, pile some Apricot and Almond Jam onto the remaining Coconut-Corn Bread to munch while enjoying the cinnamon-flavoured Mocha Coffee.

Apricot and Almond Jam

250g (8oz) dried apricots	*4 cups sugar*
2 cups water	*¼ cup slivered almonds*
	¼ cup lemon juice

1 Soak the apricots overnight in the water. The next day simmer in the same water until tender, about 20 minutes.

2 Add the sugar, almonds and lemon juice. Bring to the boil, stirring until the sugar has dissolved. Continue boiling, stirring frequently, until setting point is reached, about 25 minutes.

3 Remove from the heat, stand for 5 minutes, then ladle the jam into hot, sterilized jars. Makes about 4 cups, plenty for this breakfast and several more to come.

Mocha Coffee

150g (5oz) cooking chocolate	*sugar*
4 tbsp milk	*6 cinnamon sticks*
freshly brewed extra-strong	*whipped cream*
coffee	*ground cinnamon*

Melt the chocolate and milk in a small saucepan, over a flame at the table if possible. Pour some coffee into each cup, then the hot chocolate. Guests add their own sugar to taste and stir it in with a cinnamon stick. Top with some whipped cream and a sprinkling of cinnamon.

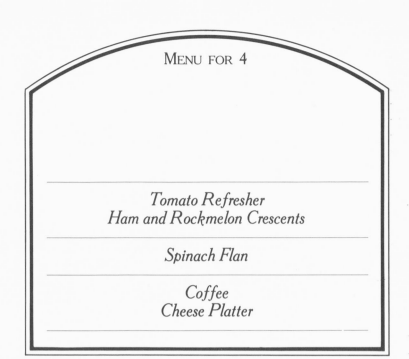

MENU FOR 4

Tomato Refresher
Ham and Rockmelon Crescents

Spinach Flan

Coffee
Cheese Platter

IF the thought of preparing pastry has ever prevented you from making a quiche or flan, now you can go ahead with confidence. Simply use 4 sheets of filo pastry and a little melted butter. Only a minute or two and no mess later you will have a pastry-lined tin just waiting to be baked. Fill it with a thick spinach custard, top it with grated cheese and you have the perfect flan, light, delicious and nutritious. The spinach and onions can be prepared the day before, leaving only the custard to be mixed in and added to the pastry at the last minute. While the flan is cooking, serve icy cold glasses of Tomato Refresher and sweet, ripe rockmelon crescents wrapped in thin slices of ham. Then, to finish, accompany your coffee with a selection of cheeses, both sweet and savoury, and some plain biscuits, pumpernickel and dried fruits.

'Fill all the glasses there, for why
Should every creature drink but I,
Why, man of morals, tell me why?'
Abraham Cowley, *Drinking*

Tomato Refresher

1 × 850ml (1 ½ pint) tin   *1 cup buttermilk*
tomato juice   *½ cucumber (about 250g; 8oz)*
2 tbsp lemon juice

Peel and roughly chop the cucumber. Place in a food processor bowl or blender with the buttermilk and blend till smooth. Pour into a jug and mix in the tomato juice. If you don't have a food processor or blender, grate the cucumber and mix with the liquids. Prepare well before required and refrigerate. On a very hot morning, pour into long glasses over ice cubes.

Ham and Rockmelon Crescents

1 small rockmelon   *2 × 125g (4oz) packets sliced leg ham*

1 Cut the rockmelon in half and scoop out the seeds. Cut each half into 5 wedges and remove the skins.
2 Wrap a piece of ham around each wedge of rockmelon and secure with a toothpick. Chill until ready to serve.

Spinach Flan

75g (2½oz) melted butter
4 sheets filo pastry
1 bunch spinach
½ tsp salt
1 tbsp butter

4 chopped shallots
2 eggs
½ cup cream
¼ tsp nutmeg
freshly ground black pepper
60g (2oz) grated tasty cheese

Prepare the Pastry

Place a 20cm (8in) flan tin on a baking tray and brush with melted butter. Fold 1 sheet of filo pastry in half and place in the flan tin, pressing onto the bottom and sides. Fold the overlapping pastry back into the tin. Brush with more melted butter. Repeat with the remaining 3 sheets of pastry. Bake blind in a hot oven (200°C; 400°F) for 10 minutes. To bake blind, place a sheet of greaseproof paper over the pastry, extending it above the sides of the tin. Fill with a layer of dried peas, beans or rice. Remove the paper and peas after baking.

Prepare the Filling

Wash and chop the spinach and place in a large saucepan with the salt. Cover tightly and cook for 10 minutes, using only the water clinging to the leaves after washing. Drain well. Melt the 1 tablespoon butter and sauté the shallots for 2 minutes. Add to the cooked spinach. Lightly beat together the eggs, cream, nutmeg and lots of pepper. Mix well into the spinach and onions.

Bake the Flan

Pour the spinach mixture into the partly cooked pastry case and sprinkle with the grated cheese. Bake in a hot oven (200°C; 400°F) for 40 minutes, until puffed and the filling has set. Stand at room temperature for a couple of minutes before removing from the tin and serving.

Cheese Platter

Browse through a cheese shop and see what you can find. Choose cheeses that offer a variety of colour and both sweet and savoury flavours. Be adventurous! Arrange your selection on a large platter with some plain biscuits or pumpernickel rounds (or both) and some dried fruits.

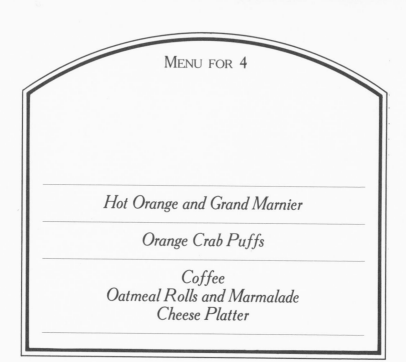

MENU FOR 4

Hot Orange and Grand Marnier

Orange Crab Puffs

Coffee
Oatmeal Rolls and Marmalade
Cheese Platter

IF you like the flavour of oranges, you'll love this breakfast —
especially on a cold and wet winter morning. Guests will instantly
respond to a cosy atmosphere and mugs of the Hot Orange and
Grand Marnier drink. Once everyone is thoroughly warm, inside and out,
progress to the Orange Crab Puffs. The crab is flavoured with mushrooms, grated orange rind and a dash of Cointreau, then piled into light,
flaky vol-au-vent cases. Finish off with copious quantities of coffee and
hot, fresh oatmeal rolls, accompanied by some of your favourite cheeses
and marmalade.

Hot Orange and Grand Marnier

2 cups weak Orange Pekoe tea   ½ cup Grand Marnier
2 cups orange juice   4 slices lemon

1 Bring the tea and orange juice to the boil in a saucepan. Remove from the heat and add the Grand Marnier.
2 Pour immediately into heated mugs over a slice of lemon.

Orange Crab Puffs

1 tbsp butter
250g (8oz) thinly sliced
    mushrooms
3 tbsp flour
300ml (½ pint) milk
1 × 200g (7oz) tin crab

30ml (1 fl oz) Cointreau
2 tsp chopped fresh rosemary or 1
    scant tsp dried
grated rind of 1 orange
4 × 100mm (4in) vol-au-vent
    cases

1 Melt the butter in a large frying pan over a medium heat. Add the mushrooms and cook until they are soft and reduced in size, about 5 minutes.
2 Stir in the flour and cook for 1 minute. Remove from the heat and gradually blend in the milk. Return to the heat and stir until boiling and thickened.
3 Drain and flake the crab. Add to the mushroom sauce with the Cointreau, rosemary and orange rind. Heat through gently.

4 Spoon the crab mixture into the pastry cases, which have been warming in a slow oven (150°C; 300°F) for 5 minutes. Serve immediately.

These Orange Crab Puffs take only 10 minutes to make if all the ingredients have been measured and prepared beforehand. However, to reduce the final cooking time even further, the mushroom sauce can be made earlier in the morning, covered and set aside. Bring to the boil again before adding the remaining ingredients just before serving.

'Oh that I were an orange-tree,
That busy plant!
Then I should ever laden be,
And never want
Some fruit for Him that dressed me.'
George Herbert, *The Temple*

Oatmeal Rolls

2 cups milk	60g (2oz) melted butter
250g (8oz) rolled oats	1 tsp salt
1 sachet dry yeast (7g / ¼oz)	2 cups wholemeal flour
1 tsp sugar	1 lightly beaten egg
¼ cup warm water	extra oats

1 Heat the milk without boiling and pour over the rolled oats in a large bowl. Soak for 1 hour.

2 Stir the yeast and sugar into the warm water. Stand for 10 to 15 minutes, until the yeast begins to froth.

3 Add the yeast mixture, butter, salt and flour to the oats, forming a dough. Knead on a board sprinkled with extra flour for 10 minutes.

4 Place the dough in a lightly oiled bowl, turn over once, and cover with plastic food wrap. Stand in a warm place until doubled in bulk, 1 to 1½ hours.

5 Punch down the dough and shape into small rolls. Place on a greased baking tray, leaving about 2cm (1in) between each roll. Cover and allow to rise again.

6 Brush the tops of the rolls with the egg and sprinkle with a few extra rolled oats. Bake in a hot oven (200°C; 400°F) for 20 minutes, until golden brown. Serve while still hot, or cool and freeze. To reheat, thaw the rolls and place in a slow oven (150°C; 300°F) for 15 to 20 minutes.

These rolls are best served with marmalade and some strongly flavoured cheese. One of the Castello varieties, a pepper or Blue Vein cheese and a matured Cheddar are good choices.

'Where there's no more bread,
boon companions melt away.'

Miguel de Cervantes, *Don Quixote*

4

Croissants and

Brioches

No book on breakfasts would be complete without recipes for croissants and brioches. To serve a traditional continental breakfast of these delicious rolls with fruit juice and coffee, it is certainly simpler to visit your nearest pâtisserie. Simpler, perhaps, but not nearly as much fun or as satisfying. Start by making your own brioches and be pleasantly surprised. These rich little rolls are made from one of the easiest of all yeast doughs. Then, as soon as you have discovered just how easy it is to make brioches, you will be ready to launch into the croissants. Don't be afraid! Though more time-consuming, they are not as daunting as they first appear. Soon your freezer will never be without one or both of these home-made delicacies, ready to heat up at a moment's notice if you simply feel like indulging yourself, or for an impromptu breakfast feast! With some cheeses and jam, fruit juice and lots of coffee you have an instant and hard-to-beat breakfast.

Then for the bonus. Once you have mastered these basic recipes, there are endless variations to try. Whether your fancy is for the sweet or more savoury flavours, you will find plenty to tempt you in the following menus.

Champagne

Brioches
Croissants
Lemon Butter, Jam, Camembert, Peach
Melba and Ski Queen cheeses

Café au Lait
Fresh Fruit

THOUGH many are as good, no breakfast can beat the basic continental meal of croissants or brioches (or both) and coffee. Not only is it delicious, it is also one of the simplest breakfasts to prepare. Just remove the required number of croissants and brioches from your freezer — and what self-respecting freezer would be without an adequate supply! — and heat them through while sipping champagne. Then take your hot rolls along with lashings of butter, some cheeses and sweet toppings and plenty of coffee, sit in the sun if possible, and pretend you are at a sidewalk café in Paris.

Brioches

Deliciously rich, light and crumbly, brioches are also very easy to make. With the assistance of a food processor, there is no kneading by hand. If you don't have a food processor or dough hook, simply follow the recipe below, rubbing the butter into the flour with your fingertips and kneading for only 2 minutes before and after the initial rising. Use the correct brioche moulds to make the traditional breakfast brioches-à-tête, the crown-shaped rolls with the small round hats.

1 sachet dry yeast (7g / ¼oz)	*1 tsp salt*
1 tbsp sugar	*125g (4oz) butter*
¼ cup warm milk	*2 large eggs*
2 cups flour	*glaze: 1 egg yolk, 1 tbsp milk*

1 Stir the yeast and sugar into the milk and leave for 10 to 15 minutes, until frothy.

2 Place the flour, salt and butter in the bowl of the food processor fitted with the metal blade. Whiz for a few seconds to distribute the butter. Add the eggs and yeast mixture and whiz again for about 30 seconds.

3 Place the dough in a lightly oiled bowl and turn over once so that the oiled side is on top. Cover with plastic food wrap and stand in a warm place until the dough has doubled in bulk, about 1 hour.

4 Punch the dough down, place in the food processor and whiz for another 30 seconds.

5 Divide the dough into 6 equal portions. For each portion, pinch off enough dough to make a ball about the size of a marble. Form the remaining dough into a larger ball and place in a greased brioche mould. With your thumb, make a small indentation in the top and sit the smaller ball in it.

6 Cover the moulds and leave to rise again, about 30 minutes. Beat together the egg and milk glaze and brush lightly over the risen brioches.

7 Bake in a moderate oven (180°C; 350°F) for 20 minutes, until a very light golden colour. Serve immediately, or cool on a wire rack and freeze for later use. When reheating, simply thaw, then place in a slow oven (150°C; 300°F) for 20 minutes.

'Besides, they always smell of bread and butter.'

Lord Byron, *Beppo*

Croissants

Croissants are lighter and flakier than brioches, and even richer in fresh, golden butter. Probably the best known breakfast roll, they require a considerable amount of patience and effort — rolling, folding, turning and resting several times — to give a result not unlike a yeast-raised puff pastry. In the following recipe this rolling, folding and turning has been minimized to yield the characteristic croissant flavour and texture without quite so much hard work. The recipe may look a little daunting. But just make a start, then follow through each step to become the proud creator of 12 fresh, delicious croissants.

1 sachet dry yeast (7g / ¼oz)	*½ cup warm milk*
1 tbsp castor sugar	*1 large egg*
¼ cup warm water	*175g (6oz) thinly sliced butter*
2½ cups flour	*glaze: 1 egg*
½ tsp salt	*2 tbsp milk*

Preparing the Dough

1 Stir the yeast and sugar into the water. Stand for 10 to 15 minutes, until frothy.

2 Sift the flour and salt. Stir in the milk, the lightly beaten egg and the yeast mixture to form a dough. Knead for 5 to 10 minutes. Place the dough in a lightly oiled bowl and turn once, so that the oiled surface is on top. Cover with plastic food wrap and leave in a warm place until doubled in bulk (about 1 hour).

Rolling the Dough

1 Turn the dough onto a lightly floured board and roll into a long rectangle about 0.5cm (¼in) thick. Mark into thirds along the longer side. Place one-third of the butter over the middle section of the dough. Fold

the unbuttered sections of dough over the centre and press the edges to seal the butter inside.

2 Repeat this step twice, using the remaining two-thirds of the butter. Roll into a rectangle and fold into thirds once more. Cover the dough with plastic and rest in the refrigerator for 30 minutes.

3 Roll the dough into a rectangle and fold as before 3 more times. Refrigerate for a further 30 minutes.

Shaping the Croissants

1 Roll the dough into a long rectangle. Cut to form 12 pieces, each about 13cm (5in) square. Beat together the egg and milk glaze and brush lightly over the squares.

2 Fold each square into a triange. Roll each triangle loosely, starting with the longest side and finishing with the point underneath. Curve into a crescent shape. You may find it easier to divide the dough in half, rolling and shaping one half into 6 croissants, then repeating with the remaining dough.

Baking the Croissants

1 Place the shaped croissants on an ungreased baking tray and brush with the glaze. Cover with a clean cloth and stand in a warm place for 30 minutes to rise.

2 Bake in a hot oven (200°C; 400°F) for 15 to 20 minutes, until lightly coloured. Do not overcook.

Serving the Croissants

1 Take to the table straight from the oven or cool and freeze. To reheat, thaw and place in a slow oven (150°C; 300°F) for 15 to 20 minutes.

2 The croissants can also be prepared the previous day. Shape them and refrigerate overnight. Stand at room temperature for 1½ hours before baking and serving.

The accompaniments

Purists claim that, for the perfect croissant or brioche, no accompaniment other than fresh, sweet butter is required. And certainly this allows full enjoyment of their flavour. However, the provision of some accompaniments can add interest and variety. Just be careful that whatever you choose is simple enough to enhance without overpowering the natural flavour of the rolls. Experiment and discover your own favourite additions. The following are ones I have found to be most popular. For both croissants and brioches a light berry jam is perfect, while the tang of lemon butter makes a different and delicious addition to your croissants.

A soft, creamy Camembert will never go astray. And for a change try one of the slightly sweeter cheeses, such as a Danish Grand Marnier or Peach Melba. While these are especially delicious on croissants, thin slices of Norwegian Ski Queen are, to my mind, and taste buds, the best possible way to enjoy a brioche.

> 'The critical period of matrimony is breakfast-time.'
> A. P. Herbert, *Uncommon Law*

Café au Lait

To complete the continental atmosphere of this meal, serve your coffee in the traditional French breakfast manner. Very large, bowl-shaped cups are used, large enough for dunking the croissants and brioches if you wish. Have 2 pots at hand, one containing hot milk and the other very strong coffee. Pour equal quantities of milk and coffee simultaneously into each cup.

> 'Look to your health; and if you have it,
> praise God, and value it next to a good
> conscience; for health is the second
> blessing that we mortals are capable of;
> a blessing that money cannot buy.'
> Izaak Walton, *Compleat Angler*

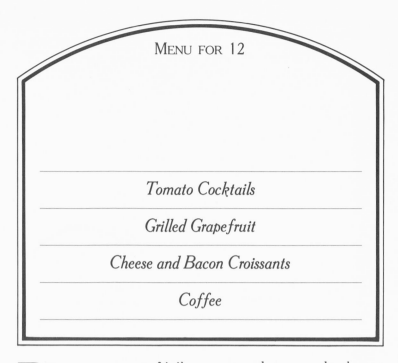

Tomato Cocktails

Grilled Grapefruit

Cheese and Bacon Croissants

Coffee

BY now, as an expert pâtissière, you are ready to proceed to the next step: croissants stuffed with cheese and bacon. Simply prepare the cheese and bacon mixture and enclose it in the croissant dough you have practised so frequently. The resulting, delightfully plump, croissants are very easy to serve. Just wrap them in large napkins and hand them to your guests. Or, if you prefer a little more formality, serve them on plates with some lightly sautéed mushrooms and a grilled tomato. Precede your croissant with tomato juice spiked with tabasco. Then, to turn this into a meal perfect for those cooler days, sprinkle grapefruit halves with some sherry and a little brown sugar before popping them under the griller to heat through.

'We arg'ed the thing at breakfast, we arg'ed the thing at tea,
And the more we arg'ed the question, the more we didn't agree.'
William Carleton, *Farm Ballads*, 'Betsy and I are out'

Tomato Cocktails

Pour chilled tomato juice into tall glasses. Add a couple of drops of tabasco to each glass, stir and serve.

Grilled Grapefruit

6 grapefruit	*12 tbsp medium sherry*	*brown sugar*

1 Prepare the grapefruit by cutting into halves and removing the cores and seeds. Then, with a very sharp knife, loosen the flesh from the skins and separate the segments. Set aside until ready to serve.
2 Sprinkle each grapefruit half with 1 tablespoon sherry and a little brown sugar. Place under a moderate griller, not too close to the flame, for a few seconds until the fruit is warm and the sugar has caramelized slightly. Be careful not to burn the sugar. Serve immediately.

' "You must sit down," says Love, "and taste My meat."
So I did sit and eat.'
George Herbert, *The Temple*, 'Love'

Cheese and Bacon Croissants

4 rashers bacon	*150g (5oz) grated tasty cheese*
basic croissant dough (see page 82) (substituting the 1 tbsp sugar with	
1 tsp sugar)	

1 Chop the bacon finely and fry till crisp. Drain on absorbent paper and cool before mixing with the grated cheese.

2 Follow the basic croissant recipe (see page 82) until the dough has been rolled and cut into squares ready for shaping.

3 Divide the cheese and bacon mixture between the 12 squares, placing a spoonful diagonally across the centre. Fold each square into a triangle over the filling, roll and shape into a crescent.

4 Allow the stuffed croissants to rise, then glaze and bake as in the basic recipe. Serve immediately or cool and freeze, ready for thawing and reheating when required.

'Many's the long night I've dreamed
of cheese — toasted, mostly.'

R. L. Stevenson, *Treasure Island*

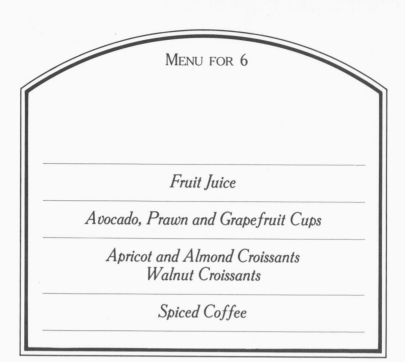

Fruit Juice

Avocado, Prawn and Grapefruit Cups

Apricot and Almond Croissants
Walnut Croissants

Spiced Coffee

HERE is a menu for those with good appetites and plenty of time. Begin with the Avocado, Prawn and Grapefruit Cups, a wonderful combination of fresh fruits and seafood flavoured with rum and brown sugar and served in the grapefruit shells. Then continue at a leisurely pace with two varieties of stuffed croissants. The first makes use of Apricot and Almond Jam from page 69. In the second, a deliciously different croissant is obtained with the combination of chopped walnuts, brown sugar and cinnamon. Finally, serve large amounts of hot, lightly spiced coffee.

'And homeless near a thousand homes I stood,
And near a thousand tables pined and wanted food.'
William Wordsworth, *Guilt and Sorrow*

Avocado, Prawn and Grapefruit Cups

3 grapefruit
2 tbsp brown sugar
1/4 cup rum

1 large avocado
150g (5oz) shelled prawns
1/2 cup shelled and halved
    pistachio nuts

1 Halve the grapefruit and carefully remove the flesh, keeping the skins intact. Cut the flesh into segments after removing all the seeds and pith. Place in a shallow bowl and sprinkle with the brown sugar and rum. Stir, cover and refrigerate overnight.
2 Before your guests arrive, peel, seed and dice the avocado. Combine with the grapefruit.
3 Just before serving, add the prawns and pistachio nuts. Pile into the reserved grapefruit shells and spoon over a little of the rum marinade.

'No human being, however great or powerful,
was ever so free as a fish.'
John Ruskin, *The Two Paths*

Apricot and Almond Croissants

1/2 basic croissant dough
    (see page 82)

6 tbsp Apricot and Almond Jam
    (see page 69)
1/2 cup flaked almonds

1 Follow the basic croissant recipe (see page 82) until the dough has been rolled and cut into squares, ready for shaping.
2 Use only 6 squares, setting aside the remaining 6 for the Walnut Croissants. Brush the squares lightly with the glaze and place 1 tablespoonful of jam diagonally across the centre of each. Fold each square into a triangle over the filling, roll and shape into a crescent.
3 Place on an ungreased baking tray and allow to rise for about 30 minutes. Brush with the glaze and sprinkle with the flaked almonds. Bake in a hot oven (200°C; 400°F) for 15 to 20 minutes.
    A word of warning: allow these croissants to cool just a little before eating as the jam centre is very hot straight from the oven!

Walnut Croissants

1 cup walnut pieces
1½ tbsp brown sugar

½ basic croissant dough (see page 82)
1 tsp cinnamon

1 Finely chop the walnuts. Reserve one quarter. Mix the remaining walnuts with the sugar and cinnamon.

2 Use the 6 squares of dough remaining from the preceding recipe. Glaze lightly and place 1 heaped tablespoon of the walnut filling diagonally across the centre of each. Fold, roll and shape as before.

3 Place on an ungreased baking tray and allow to rise. Brush with the glaze and sprinkle with the reserved finely chopped walnuts. Bake with the Apricot and Almond Croissants.

As with all stuffed croissants, both of these are very easy to serve and eat, requiring no extra butter or spreads. In fact, all you do need is your fingers, large napkins so no crumbs are wasted, and a hearty appetite. Thus, they are a perfect breakfast to serve large numbers of guests. Simply make and freeze several batches of croissants at your leisure. Then, at breakfast-time, be free to mingle with your guests, leaving the croissants to warm through in the oven.

Spiced Coffee

Make fresh coffee in your favourite manner, adding the spices to the water before brewing. For each 6 cups of coffee use 2 cinnamon sticks and 6 cloves. Sweeten if desired with brown sugar and, for those who prefer their coffee white, provide thick pouring cream.

'Look here, Steward, if this is coffee, I want tea;
but if this is tea, then I wish for coffee.'

Punch, 1902

Champagne with Grand Marnier

Scrambled Eggs in Wholemeal Brioches

Fresh Fruit with Ricotta-Orange Dip

Viennese-style Coffee

THIS menu has a distinct orange theme. Grand Marnier is featured in both the champagne to begin and later in the Ricotta-Orange Dip. In between, eggs scrambled with a little orange juice and flavoured with grated orange rind are piled into crisp, warm wholemeal brioche shells. Before your guests arrive simply thaw the brioches, which have been made in the preceding days, and remove most of the soft centres. Later the shells need only be warmed through in the oven while the eggs are scrambling. You can, of course, buy your brioches. However, this home-made wholemeal variety gives a crisper, more flavoursome result, perfectly complementing the soft delicacy of the scrambled eggs. To finish, serve coffee in the Viennese style, mixed with milk and topped with lightly whipped cream.

> 'Oh, my friends, be warned by me,
> That breakfast, dinner, lunch and tea,
> Are all the human frame requires . . .'
> Hilaire Belloc, *Cautionary Tales*, 'Henry King'

Champagne with Grand Marnier

Begin with a tablespoon or two of Grand Marnier in each glass. Top up with your favourite champagne.

Scrambled Eggs in Wholemeal Brioches

Wholemeal Brioches

7g (¼oz) dry yeast	1 tsp salt
1 tsp sugar	125g (4oz) butter
⅓ cup warm milk	2 large eggs
2 cups wholemeal flour	glaze: 1 egg yolk
2 tbsp gluten flour	1 tbsp milk

Make the brioches using the basic brioche method (see page 81). Cool and freeze until required.

Scrambled Eggs

6 wholemeal brioches	3 tbsp butter
12 large eggs	grated rind of 1 orange
juice of 1 orange	freshly ground black pepper

1 Prepare the brioches. Thaw the brioches. Cut a slice from the top (including the small 'hat') and pull out most of the soft centre. Place the shells and tops in a very slow oven (100°C; 200°F) while the eggs are scrambling. By the time eggs are ready, the brioches will be hot and beautifully crisp.

2 Scramble the eggs. Very lightly beat together the eggs and orange juice. Melt the butter in a large saucepan over a moderate heat. Add the eggs and stir continuously with a wooden spoon until they are just beginning to set, about 10 to 12 minutes. Do not overcook. Remove from the heat and stir in three quarters of the grated orange rind and plenty of pepper. Spoon into the warmed brioche shells and sprinkle with the remaining orange rind. Lean the brioche tops against the filled shells and take straight to the table and your guests.

'Orange bright,
Like golden lamps on a green night.'
Andrew Marvell, *Bermudas*

Fresh Fruit with Ricotta-Orange Dip

200g (7oz) ricotta cheese   *3 tbsp Grand Marnier*
½ cup yoghurt   *grated orange rind*
2 tbsp castor sugar   *large chunks of fresh seasonal fruit*

1 Beat the cheese and yoghurt together, then mix in the sugar and Grand Marnier. Pile into a glass bowl and sprinkle with the grated orange rind. Cover and chill until ready to serve.

2 Place the bowl of chilled Ricotta-Orange Dip on a large platter and surround with the fresh fruits, the more colourful the better. Provide small forks or toothpicks for dipping the fruit.

'What beautiful fruit! I love fruit when it's expensive.'

Sir Arthur Wing Pinero, *The Second Mrs Tanqueray*

Viennese-style Coffee

Pour very strong black coffee and hot milk simultaneously into each cup, in the ratio of 2 parts coffee to 1 part milk. Sweeten according to taste then top with a good dollop of lightly whipped cream.

Orange Juice

Fresh Fruit Compote with Yoghurt and Honey

Bacon and Onion Buns

Iced Lemon Tea

PERFECT for the poolside, or wherever the entertaining is most relaxed, this menu makes an ideal summer breakfast. Begin with orange juice and follow it with a compote of fresh summer fruits, flavoured with Grand Marnier and topped with a dollop of yoghurt and drizzle of honey. Then just pass around some large paper napkins and baskets of Bacon and Onion Buns, fresh from the oven. Inspired by the Russian piroshki, these buns are almost as easy to make as they are to eat. Simply enclose a savoury filling of fried bacon and onions in rich wholemeal brioche dough, and bake. For a refreshing finale to your meal, and maintaining the Russian influence, serve long glasses of Iced Lemon Tea

' "Well," said Pooh, "What I like best — " and then
he had to stop and think. Because although
Eating Honey was a very good thing to do, there
was a moment just before you began to eat it which
was better than when you were, but he didn't know
what it was called.'

A. A. Milne, *The House At Pooh Corner*

Fresh Fruit Compote with Yoghurt and Honey

½ ripe pawpaw	1 punnet raspberries or strawberries
2 peaches	Grand Marnier
2 kiwi fruit	2 × 200ml (7oz) tubs yoghurt
	honey

1 Peel, seed and dice the pawpaw and peaches. Peel the kiwi fruit, halve lengthways and slice. Wash the raspberries. If using strawberries, wash, hull and cut in half unless very small.
2 Divide the fruit between 6 small glass dishes and add a slurp of Grand Marnier, the size of the slurp depending on the state of your pocket and on your taste: 1 dessertspoon to 1 tablespoon is a reasonable amount. Cover and chill until time to serve.
3 Top each compote with a good dollop of yoghurt and a drizzle of honey just before serving.

Bacon and Onion Buns

1 quantity Wholemeal Brioche dough (see page 92)	150g (5oz) bacon
	poppy seeds
125g (4oz) onions	sesame seeds

1 Finely chop the onions and bacon and place in a cold frying pan. Turn the heat to medium and cook, stirring frequently, until the onions are soft and a light golden colour (about 15 minutes). Drain on absorbent paper and allow to cool.
2 Prepare the Wholemeal Brioche dough (see page 92) until the dough has risen once.
3 Punch the dough and divide into 12 equal pieces. Roll each piece into a ball then flatten to make a thin circle. Place 1 heaped teaspoon of the bacon and onion mixture in the centre of each circle and form the dough into a ball around the filling. Place the buns on a greased baking tray, cover and allow to double in size (about 30 minutes).
4 Lightly beat the egg yolk and milk and brush over the buns. Sprinkle half the buns with the poppy seeds and half with the sesame seeds. Bake in a moderately hot oven (190°C; 375°F) for 20 minutes. Serve straight from the oven.

The buns can be prepared the previous day and refrigerated overnight. Allow to rise at room temperature for at least 1 hour before baking and serving. Or bake and freeze the buns in the preceding days or weeks. Thaw in the morning, then reheat in a slow oven (150°C; 300°F) for 20 minutes.

Iced Lemon Tea

freshly brewed, weak tea
sugar
1 thinly sliced lemon

2 tbsp lightly crushed mint leaves
extra lemon slices
small sprigs of mint
ice cubes

1 Place the sliced lemon and crushed mint leaves into a large glass jug. Pour over the hot, freshly brewed, very weak tea. Sweeten sparingly if desired — no more than 1 to 2 tablespoons of sugar. Cover and cool at room temperature before chilling in the refrigerator.

2 To serve, place some ice cubes in a tall glass. Pour over the chilled tea and decorate with an extra slice of lemon and a sprig of mint.

'I eat well, and I drink well, and I sleep well—
but that's all.'
Thomas Morton, *A Roland for an Oliver*

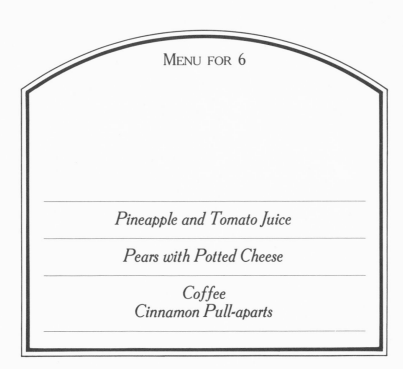

Pineapple and Tomato Juice

Pears with Potted Cheese

Coffee
Cinnamon Pull-aparts

O N a hot morning try this very refreshing breakfast. Begin with well chilled glasses of Pineapple and Tomato Juice, a perfect way to quench an early or mid-morning thirst and to freshen the palate for what is to come. Continue with cold, juicy pears topped with the deliciously contrasting sharpness of potted cheese. And to accompany your coffee offer warm, spicy Cinnamon Pull-aparts — a filling of cinnamon, walnuts and sultanas, lightly sweetened with brown sugar and rolled in the wholemeal brioche dough.

'Botticelli isn't a wine, you Juggins! Botticelli's a cheese.'
Punch, 1894

Pineapple and Tomato Juice

Simply mix equal quantities of pineapple and tomato juice and chill well. Serve in long glasses over ice cubes.

> 'Bachelor's fare: bread and cheese, and kisses.'
> Johnathon Swift, *Polite Conversation*

Pears with Potted Cheese

1 cup grated tasty cheese	*1 tbsp finely chopped chives*
50g (2oz butter)	*½ tsp dried thyme*
2 tbsp dry sherry or vermouth	*freshly ground black pepper*
1 tbsp finely chopped parsley	*6 medium-sized firm, ripe pears*

dill or parsley to garnish

1 Make the potted cheese. Beat together the cheese, butter and sherry or vermouth. Add the herbs and lots of pepper and beat again. Place in a jar or pottery container, cover and refrigerate for several days to allow the flavours to develop.

2 Prepare the pears. In the morning, halve and core the pears. Brush the exposed surfaces with lemon juice to prevent browning. If necessary, cut a small slice from the bottom of each half to allow it to sit firmly on a plate. Chill until required.

3 To serve the pears. Remove the potted cheese from the refrigerator half an hour before required. Arrange 2 pear halves on each plate and place a good spoonful of potted cheese in the cavities made when the cores were removed. Garnish with a sprig of fresh dill or parsley and serve.

Cinnamon Pull-aparts

1 quantity Wholemeal Brioche
dough (see page 92)
2 tbsp melted butter

⅓ cup brown sugar
2 tsp cinnamon
½ cup chopped walnuts
½ cup sultanas

1 Follow the recipe for making Wholemeal Brioches until the dough has risen once.

2 Punch the dough down and roll into a rectangle about 46 × 23cm (18 × 9ins). Brush with the melted butter. Mix together the brown sugar and cinnamon and spread over the dough surface. Scatter the walnuts and sultanas over the top.

3 Roll the dough like a Swiss roll, from the long side. Cut into 12 even slices and pack into a greased 20cm (8in) round cake tin, placing 9 slices around the edge and 3 in the centre. Cover and allow to rise again, about 30 minutes.

4 Bake in a hot oven (200°C; 400°F) for 20 minutes. Serve immediately or cool and freeze for later use. To reheat, thaw and place in a slow oven (150°C; 300°F) for 20 minutes.

'I won't quarrel with my bread and butter.'

Jonathan Swift, *Polite Conversation*

5

Picnics

Smoked Oyster and Onion Quiche
102

Homemade Rye Bread
Chicken Liver Pâté with Port
Liptauer Cheese
106

The Giant Sausage Sizzle
110

DON'T limit your breakfasts to indoors — in fact, you needn't stay around the house at all. Pack a picnic and go wherever your fancy takes you — straight to your favourite spot or just hop in the car and discover somewhere new. Or even take a bus or train and a short walk to reach that perfect picnic site. A portable ice box and a basket or two are usually all that is required to provide you with good food in an atmosphere perfectly designed to relax your tensions, refresh your spirits and stimulate good companionship.

'Here with a Loaf of Bread beneath the bough,
A Flask of Wine, a Book of Verse — and Thou
Beside me singing in the Wilderness —
And Wilderness is Paradise now.'
Edward Fitzgerald, *Omar Khayyam*

Champagne and Orange Juice

Smoked Oyster and Onion Quiche
Mixed Vegetable Pickles
Walnut Cheese Loaves

Coffee
Fresh Fruit

MAKE the most of the sun and the great outdoors with this no-fuss picnic. A week or two before make the easy Mixed Vegetable Pickles. Then, two days before, whip up the walnut cheese in your food processor or electric mixer and assemble the loaves. Finally, the day before your picnic, make the quiche and prepare the fruit. Everything is then ready to pop into your ice box the next morning, along with a bottle of champagne and some orange juice. Fill a vacuum flask with freshly brewed coffee, pack a bundle of large napkins, a knife to cut the quiche and the Walnut Cheese Loaves, a fork to extract the pickles — then off to find a sunny spot. No other knives, forks or plates are required, simply your fingers, some napkins and a good appetite!

'A very ancient and fish-like smell.'
Shakespeare, *The Tempest*

Smoked Oyster and Onion Quiche

Pastry Crumb Case

1¼ cups wholemeal flour	100g (3½oz) grated tasty cheese
¼ tsp cayenne pepper	75g (2½oz) softened butter

1 Mix together the flour, cayenne and cheese in a bowl. Rub in the butter with your fingertips.
2 Press the crumb mixture into the base and sides of an ungreased 20cm (8in) springform tin. Chill until ready to use.

Smoked Oyster and Onion Filling

3 medium onions	⅓ cup milk
25g (1oz) butter	3 eggs
1 × 105g (3½oz) tin smoked oysters	75g (2½oz) grated tasty cheese
200ml (7oz) tub yoghurt	2 tbsp chopped chives
	freshly ground black pepper
1 tsp paprika	

1 Chop the onions. Melt the butter in a frying pan and sauté the onions until golden, about 3 minutes. Drain on absorbent paper.
2 Drain and chop the smoked oysters.
3 Combine the yoghurt, milk and eggs. Stir in the cheese, chives and a good grinding of pepper.
4 Spread the cooked onions over the pastry, then the chopped oysters. Pour the egg mixture over the top and sprinkle with paprika.
5 Bake in a hot oven (200°C; 400°F) for 40 minutes. Cool, chill and transport to your picnic in the tin.

Mixed Vegetable Pickles

250g (8oz) green beans	250g (8oz) zucchini (courgettes)
250g (8oz) carrots	1 large red capsicum (pepper)
250g (8oz) cauliflower sprigs	garlic cloves
	sprigs of fresh oregano

1 Cut the beans into 2cm (1in) lengths. Cut the carrots into 0.5cm (¼in) rounds and break the cauliflower into small sprigs.
2 Cut the zucchini into 0.5cm (¼in) slices. Cut the capsicum into quarters and remove the seeds. Slice lengthways into 0.5cm (¼in) strips.
3 Quarter fill a large saucepan with water and bring to the boil. Add the beans, carrots and cauliflower, cover and return to the boil. Lower the heat and simmer for 3 minutes. Drain and refresh under cold water.
4 Again bring the saucepan, with about 2cm (1in) water, to the boil. Add the capsicum and zucchini, cover and return to the boil. Drain immediately and refresh under cold water.
5 Place a clove of garlic in the bottom of each sterilized jar to be used. Arrange the vegetables in the jars and insert a sprig of oregano into the side of each one.
6 Pour the pickling solution over the vegetables and seal. Leave at least 24 hours before serving. They will keep in the refrigerator for several weeks.

Pickling Solution

2 cups white vinegar	2 tsp mustard seeds
2 cups water	2 tsp peppercorns
2 tsp salt	4 tbsp olive oil

Mix all the ingredients together well and pour over the prepared vegetables.

' "A loaf of bread," the Walrus said,
"Is what we chiefly need:
Pepper and vinegar besides
Are very good indeed —
Now if you're ready, oysters dear,
We can begin to feed." '
Lewis Carroll, *Through the Looking Glass*

Walnut Cheese Loaves

These loaves are best made a couple of days before required to allow the flavours time to develop fully. The creaminess of the cheese teams well with the fruit and coffee and is a perfect finale to the stronger flavours of the quiche and pickles.

---

125 (4oz) Camembert
125g (4oz) cream cheese
2 tbsp unsalted butter
2 tbsp port

½ cup chopped walnuts
freshly ground black pepper
2 bread sticks (mixed grain are best)

---

1 Have the cheeses and butter at room temperature. Beat together in an electric mixer or combine in your food processor. Add the port and mix well. Stir in the walnuts and plenty of pepper.

2 Cut the bread sticks in half lengthwise. Pull out most of the soft centre from each half, leaving a shell about 1cm (½in) thick. Press the walnut cheese mixture into the hollows, reassemble the loaves, wrap in aluminium foil and refrigerate.

3 Chill until ready to eat. Slice into 2cm (1in) rounds just before serving, or slice before leaving for your picnic, reassemble the loaves and wrap again in aluminium foil until serving time.

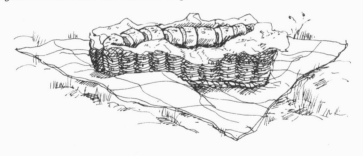

MENU FOR 6 UPWARDS
The Civilized Picnic

Champagne

Home-made Rye Bread
Schinkenbrot
Sweet and Sour Bread
Rye Crispbreads

Chicken Liver Pâté with Port
Liptauer Cheese
Pickles and Stuffed Olives
Jarlsberg and Brie Cheese

Coffee and Fresh Fruit

FOLLOW this recipe for a perfect morning. Take a selection of breads and some pâté, cheeses and pickles. Combine with vacuum flasks of hot coffee and plenty of fresh fruit. Add bottles of champagne, good friends and a sunny day, and your recipe is complete.

The ingredients following will serve from 6 to 12 people very adequately. If you want to invite more, simply add one or two extra varieties of bread and some additional cheeses. Spread everything out on a cloth under the trees, pour the champagne and enjoy a relaxed and civilized morning.

'And we meet, with champagne and chicken, at last.'
Lady Mary Wortley Montagu, *Letters and Works*, 'The Lover'

Home-made Rye Bread

Unlike most dark, richly flavoured rye breads, this one has a good, light texture, thanks to the gluten flour. Also, thanks to the gluten flour, the kneading time is minimized, making this bread well within the scope of those not accustomed to baking their own. If you have a food processor or dough hook, the operation is simplified even further. However, even if you don't possess one of these gadgets, do make the bread. The satisfaction you will achieve from seeing the beautiful, round loaf, the delicious aroma of baking bread that will pervade your home, and the praise of your friends will certainly make the effort worthwhile.

1½ sachets dry yeast (10g/⅓oz)　*1 tsp salt*
100ml (3½fl oz) warm water　*1 dsp carraway seeds*
150ml (5fl oz) boiling water　*1 tbsp polenta*
1 tbsp butter　*150g (5oz) rye flour*
2 tbsp molasses　*150g (5oz) wholemeal flour*
75g (2½oz) gluten flour

---

1 Dissolve the yeast in the warm water. Set aside for 10 to 15 minutes, until the yeast begins to froth.
2 In a large bowl, pour the boiling water over the butter, molasses, salt and carraway seeds, and stir until the butter has dissolved.
3 Add the polenta, the flours and the yeast mixture to the liquid, stirring to form a stiff dough. Knead on a lightly floured board for 5 to 10 minutes, until the dough is smooth and elastic. Place in a lightly oiled bowl and turn over once so the oiled surface is on top. Cover with plastic food wrap and leave to double in bulk, about 1½ hours.
4 Punch the dough down and knead for a couple of minutes. Form into a round loaf and place on a greased baking tray. Cover and allow to rise again, about 1 hour.
5 Bake in a moderate oven (180°C; 350°F) for 40 to 45 minutes. Cool on a wire rack. Slice when cold, wrap well in plastic and transport to the picnic. Or, for greater effect, leave whole and slice on the spot.

The bread can be made well ahead of time, frozen either sliced or whole and then thawed when required.

Bread Baskets

Place the whole loaf of Home-made Rye Bread on a round wooden board and give it pride of place at your picnic. Then, for variety, add some baskets of Schinkenbrot and Latvian Sweet and Sour breads, both available pre-sliced from your supermarket or delicatessen. Schinkenbrot is a slightly denser, moist and richly flavoured bread; the Sweet and Sour offers a lighter colour along with its distinctive taste. Finally, for a contrast of texture, add some rye or wholewheat crispbreads.

'The lion and the unicorn
Were fighting for the crown;
The lion beat the unicorn
All round the town.
Some gave them white bread,
And some gave them brown;
And some gave them plum cake
And sent them out of town.'
Nursery Rhyme

Chicken Liver Pâté with Port

This delicious pâté is one of the quickest and easiest to make, and also one of the least rich. Make it a day or two before required to allow the flavours to develop fully. Cover the top with a layer of melted ghee and it will keep in the refrigerator for at least a couple of weeks.

500g (1lb) chicken livers
1 tbsp butter
1 peeled and chopped clove garlic
2 tbsp butter
pinch mixed spice

1 tsp finely chopped fresh oregano or a good pinch dried
½ tsp salt
freshly ground black pepper
4 tbsp port

1 Sauté the livers in 1 tablespoon butter over a low to medium heat for about 4 minutes. They should still be slightly pink inside.

2 Place the livers along with any liquid and scrapings from the pan into a blender or food processor. Add the garlic, 2 tablespoons butter, mixed spice, oregano, salt and plenty of pepper, and whizz until smooth. Add the port and whizz for a few more seconds.

3 Pour the pâté into pottery moulds and smooth the surface. This mixture will fill 2 normal-sized ramekin dishes. To keep the pâté more than a day or two, melt some ghee in a saucepan and pour over the top. Make sure the ghee is not too hot or it will fry the surface of the pâté. Refrigerate until ready to transport to your picnic.

4 To serve, run the point of a sharp knife around the edge of the ramekins and lift off the ghee 'lid'.

Liptauer Cheese

Liptauer cheese has a creamy, smooth texture and flavour, studded with a variety of unusual and tasty additives. Its unique and delicious taste is well matched by its eye-catching appearance — log-shaped, delicately coloured pink by a sprinkling of paprika and surrounded by colourful pickles, stuffed green olives and sprigs of parsley.

500g (1 lb) ricotta cheese	*2 tbsp currants*
3 tbsp softened butter	*2 tbsp chopped black olives*
2 tsp grainy French mustard	*pinch cayenne pepper*
2 tsp carraway seeds	*garnish: paprika, stuffed green*
2 tbsp drained and chopped	*olives, dill pickles and parsley*
capers	*sprigs*

1 Beat together the cheese and butter till completely blended. Stir in the remaining ingredients.

2 Form the cheese into a log on a rectangular platter or in a long tupperware container. Sprinkle the top well with paprika and surround with pimento-stuffed olives, quartered dill pickles and sprigs of parsley.

Fruit Juice

Wholemeal Lebanese Bread
Breakfast, Chicken, Spicy Mexican and
Bratwurst Sausages
Chutney, Relish, Mustards, Pickles and
Horseradish

Barbecue-baked Bananas
Barbecued Corn

Coffee and Cheese Shortbread

HERE is a chance to make the most of the outdoors with an expand-able and very versatile feast. The more participants you have, the more fun you will no doubt find it! Just vary the amount of sausages you buy according to the number of guests invited. And don't only limit yourself to the sausages suggested here. Hunt around and see what other varieties you can find: Brockwurst, Weinwurst, curry, tomato and onion, Kransky and Italian-style sausages are just a few of the possibilities, making use of a variety of meats and spices.

Use your imagination as well in choosing the condiments. Try both a fruity and a tomato chutney, a relish, such as corn or zucchini, and some pickles. Of course, mustard is essential: a good hot English mustard, a grainy French one and perhaps a sweeter German variety. And don't forget the horseradish. As you can see, the more guests you invite the greater the variety of both sausages and condiments you can introduce.

'Good company and good discourse
are the very sinews of virtue.'
Izaak Walton, *Compleat Angler*

The Giant Sausage Sizzle

One of the greatest advantages of this breakfast is its simplicity. Just fill a portable ice box with your choices of sausages and plenty of fruit juice. Then load the condiments, several packets of Wholemeal Lebanese bread (for extra flavour and goodness) and some paper napkins into a basket. And be sure to remember your vaccum flasks of hot coffee and the cheese shortbread. Add a large picnic rug or two and head for the bush, checking first to be sure there are no fire bans.

> 'She stood breast high amid the corn,
> Clasp'd by the golden light of morn,
> Like the sweetheart of the sun,
> Who many a glowing kiss had won.'
>
> Thomas Hood, *Ruth*

Once you have found the perfect spot, set your fire, start on the orange juice and wait for the sausages to cook. Then tear off a piece of Lebanese bread, insert your sausage and top it with your choice of condiment. Experiment with as many different combinations of sausages and condiments as your appetite allows. Supply also some lettuce and slices of tomato which, added to the bread and sausages or just eaten on their own, provide a crispness and freshness your guests will appreciate.

After so much bread, spicy sausages and condiments, the sweetness of baked bananas and the juicy freshness of barbecued corn will be a welcome addition.

This 'breakfast' is best begun in the late morning and continued at a leisurely pace — to allow both the time and the appetite to enjoy the different food combinations offered and the peaceful surroundings. With the addition of the lettuce and fresh tomato, and the bananas and corn,

the meal provides all your nutritional requirements for the day. So linger through lunch time, into the afternoon and even on into the evening. Stop only when the day as well as the food has finished. Then return home refreshed and replete.

> 'It frequently breakfasts at 5 o'clock tea
> And dines on the following day.'
>
> Lewis Carroll, *The Hunting of the Snark*

Barbecue-baked Bananas

Choose firm, slightly green bananas, allowing at least one per person. Throw them, skin and all, into the hot coals or flames for about 10 minutes. By then the skins should just begin to show signs of splitting and the flesh will be hot and sweet, softening on the outside while still retaining some firmness in the centre. How to eat a baked banana is a matter of individual taste. Squeeze it into a piece of bread and add a sausage or any other topping you like. Or, best of all, just break open the skin and scoop out the deliciously hot, sweet flesh with a spoon.

Barbecued Corn

For ease of eating, prepare your corn at home by removing the husks and all the silk, then wrapping each cob in aluminium foil. If your corn is young and tender it will take only 15 minutes to grill over a hot flame, turning once. Hold the whole cooked cob in your hand (protected by a paper napkin), peel back the foil, add a good pat of butter . . . and eat!

> 'The corn was springing fresh and green,
> And the lark sang loud and high,
> And the red was on your lip, Mary,
> And the love-light in your eye.'
>
> Helen Selina Blackwood, Lady Dufferin, *Lament of the Irish Emigrant*

Cheese Shortbread

Conclude your Giant Sausage Sizzle with coffee brewed that morning and transported in vacuum flasks, so that it is still piping hot. To go with it try this easy-to-make cheese shortbread.

1½ cups wholemeal flour
¼ tsp dry mustard
¼ tsp cayenne pepper
125g (4oz) softened butter

1 cup grated tasty cheese
⅓ cup grated Parmesan cheese
1 lightly beaten egg
poppy seeds

1 Combine the flour, mustard and cayenne in a bowl. Rub in the butter with your fingertips. Stir in the cheeses, then the egg to form a dough. This can also be done quickly and easily in a food processor.

2 Press the dough into a greased Swiss roll tin and sprinkle with poppy seeds. Refrigerate for 1 hour.

3 Bake at 200°C (400°F) for 15 minutes, or until crisp and golden. Cool in the tin before cutting into fingers. Store in an airtight container.

A Note on
Tea and Coffee

TEA and coffee are not merely beverages to serve at the end of a meal. They are the culmination of a well planned and executed menu. As such, considerable care is necessary in their choice and preparation. Here are some hints to help you choose your tea and coffee, to brew them to obtain the maximum flavour and aroma, and to serve them with flair.

Tea

Originating in the Orient, tea was first brought to Europe as the drink of the nobility. Today, although enjoyed by everyone, it still retains its aura of ceremony and gentility. Maintaining the traditions of the Japanese tea ceremony and the English tea gardens of the last century, you too can serve your tea with style.

> 'Tea, although an Oriental,
> Is a gentleman at least;
> Cocoa is a cad and coward,
> Cocoa is a vulgar beast.'
>
> G. K. Chesterton, *The Song of Right and Wrong*

The first step in making a perfect brew is to choose the tea best suited to the occasion. To assist, there are several well-known brands offering a variety of teas, all of excellent quality. For breakfast, forget the lighter and scented varieties in favour of those with a rich, full-bodied flavour.

Darjeeling, with its muscatel-like flavour, acclaimed by many connoisseurs as the finest tea of all, would be a perfect choice. Consider also a Pure Ceylon with its full, round taste, or the rich, smoky flavour of Lapsang Souchong. Russian Caravan tea, originally transported by caravan to the imperial court of Russia, has the brisk pungency of the best of China's black teas. And, of course, do not neglect the English and Irish Breakfast blends, which combine some of the finest teas to give a traditionally British, strong and full-bodied flavour.

With these in mind visit a good tea stockist, browse through the selection and, with an adventurous spirit, sample several varieties, noting the subtleties in colour, flavour and aroma. Having chosen your tea, be sure to store it well away from other foods: it is easily tainted.

Now you are ready to make that perfect cup of tea — and thereby to establish your reputation as cook and host or hostess. Just follow these instructions:

1 Use an earthenware or porcelain pot, one which has never seen soap or detergent.

2 If possible use rain water, considered the ideal for tea making. However, if rain water is not available you can still achieve a high standard if your water is freshly drawn. Avoid using preboiled water.

3 When the water is almost boiling pour enough into the pot to heat it well. Empty the pot and add your tea. One teaspoon per cup is a good guide, to be added to or subtracted from according to your own tastes.

4 Pour on the water immediately it begins to boil and set aside to draw. Brewing time varies slightly with different varieties of tea, those with smaller leaves requiring a shorter time. For most teas 5 minutes is perfect to release the flavoursome and aromatic oils.

Now simply take the pot to the table, where all is in readiness: cups and accompaniments prepared and your guests expectant. Provide fresh milk and sugar for those with traditional English tastes. Offer also thin slices of lemon or lime, with extra hot water to dilute the tea as required. And for the more adventurous supply jam, a teaspoonsful to be added to black tea in the popular Russian style.

> 'A hardened and shameless tea drinker, who has
> for 20 years diluted his meals with only the
> infusion of this fascinating plant; whose kettle
> has scarcely time to cool; who with tea amuses
> the evening, with tea solaces the midnight, and
> with tea welcomes the morning.'
>
> Samuel Johnson, review in the *Literary Magazine*, 1757

Coffee

Coffee was first recognized growing on the hills of northern Africa. There the beans were chewed, usually by monks to increase their alterness during long evening prayer vigils. Before long the more palatable method of boiling the whole beans in water was discovered; then, in the thirteenth century, the roasting and grinding of beans before infusion commenced. From that time coffee spread rapidly through the Islamic world, Europe and finally the Americas. The growth of coffee's popularity, however, was not all smooth. For many years it was banned by Catholic and Mohammedan leaders because of its stimulant qualities. And in many places it was prohibited as a seditious beverage, being consumed in coffee houses where the intelligentsia gathered to discuss politics and foment unrest!

> 'Or to some coffee house I stray,
> For news the manna of a day,
> And from the hipp'd discourses gather
> That politics go by the weather.'
> Matthew Greene, *The Spleen*

Like tea, the making of the perfect cup of coffee is a true art, an art readily attainable by all with just a little practice and dedication. Attention should first be paid to the choice of coffee. Here the coffee lover's best friend is the specialist retailer who can guide in selecting the blend of beans and the roast most suited to individual tastes. Indeed, coffee blending is a highly individual art, allowing an infinite number of combinations. Most important in achieving your ideal blend is choosing the correct roast: light, medium, full or high, each succeeding roast giving a stronger and ultimately more bitter flavour.

Next, consider the bean itself. Today we have a wealth of high quality beans from diverse areas of the globe, each with its own distinct character. The variety of beans and subleties of flavour are too numerous to do credit to here. Be guided by your expert retailer and experiment with as many combinations as possible to open up a new world of coffee enjoyment.

Once provided with your choice of freshly roasted coffee, you must treat it with care. Buy only in small quantities as the beans quickly lose their distinctive aroma and flavour. Be sure to keep them dry; an airtight glass container is excellent. And, for the best results, grind your own beans immediately before use. Once the beans are ground the flavour and aroma are lost even more rapidly.

The final step in achieving the perfect cup of coffee is to select your method of brewing. Whichever of the many methods you decide on, the cardinal rule is never to boil your coffee. Hence the percolator is not recommended. Among the most popular methods are those using the filter principle. Whether it be simply a cone lined with filter paper and standing over a jug of hot water or one of the new electic dripolator machines, you will obtain a smooth, well rounded result. Be sure to use finely ground beans in the proportion of one tablespoon per cup.

Also popular is the infusion method of brewing. The plunger pot is the most common infuser. However, a similar result can be achieved by steeping the grounds for three to four minutes in an earthenware pot, just as you do your tea. Pour the coffee through a fine mesh strainer. Both these methods require a medium to coarse grind to give a full, rich flavour.

For a stronger, Italian-style coffee try some espresso. Special two tier pots are readily available, in which steam and water are forced through a coffee-filled basket to make a thick, aromatic brew.

Finally, for the thick, syrupy Turkish-style coffee, pulverized beans can be brewed in an *ibrik* or, failing that, in any small saucepan.

Like all culinary endeavours, approach your coffee making with a sense of adventure. Vary your choice of beans, roast and brewing method to suit the occasion. Vary also your method of serving. Try the favourite French breakfast drink of *café-au-lait*, or indulge yourself with a Viennese-style coffee smothered in freshly whipped cream. From the Mediterranean you can add any number of spices, including cinnamon, cardamon or cloves. Or try the popular Mexican combination of coffee and melted chocolate topped with whipped cream. You can even take a hint from the Caribbean and add some coconut milk, sugar and a sprinkling of toasted coconut for an unusual but tasty cup.

'I have measured out my life in coffee spoons.'
T. S. Eliot, *The Love Song of J. Alfred Prufrock*

Weights and Measures

Both metric and imperial measures are provided. Use either metric or imperial measures: do not use a mixture of both.

1 cup = 250ml
1 tablespoon = 20ml
1 teaspoon = 5ml

Cup Measurements for Solids

Flour	1 cup = 150g (5oz)
Sugar	1 cup = 250g (8oz)
Wheatgerm	1 cup = 90g (3oz)
Polenta	1 cup = 175g (6oz)
Cheese	1 cup = 125g (4oz)

Oven Temperatures

Description	°C (Celsius)	°F (Farenheit)
Very slow	100	200
Slow	150	300
Moderate	180	350
Moderately hot	190	375
Hot	200	400

Liquid Measures

Ml (millilitres)	fl.oz. (fluid ounces)
30	1
100	3
150	5
250	8
500	16

Weights

g (grams)	oz (ounces)
30	1
125	4
250	8
375	12
500	16 (1lb)

Index

A

B

C

D

G

H

IK

LM

Designed by Martin Hendry

Typeset by Savage & Co. Pty Ltd, Brisbane
Printed and bound by Globe Press, Melbourne